ISBN 9 781734 443509

INTRO TO PRODUCTION ACCOUNTING: THE CLERK

*A guide to starting out
in an accounting department
in the entertainment industry*

*Many, many thanks to Deana Bryden, Isabella Frederiksen,
Stephanie Mitchell, Max Schouweiler, Andrea Simon,
Darryl Sinclair, and Gregory Van Zuyen
for your notes and contributions.*

Much love and future success in your careers.

*Special thank you also to Dete Meserve for educating me
on the process of publishing a book, and to Avi Levy and Gavin Franks
for always calling me back to answer my questions
while I was climbing my career ladder.*

*Many thanks to SAG-AFTRA and Media Services
for their contributions.*

Introduction

Have you been thinking about what it would be like to work in accounting in the entertainment industry, but don't know where to start?

Then this book is for you.

I want to start out by saying that this is only how *I* run my department. Everyone has their own systems, and the more you work, the more you will pick up different ways of doing things the way *you* like. So please don't go around saying, "Well, in the production accounting book, it says to do it this way." NEVER SAY THAT TO A PRODUCTION ACCOUNT-ANT. *Not if you value your life.* Use what you learn in this book, but understand that every show you work on will teach you something new.

So if I can't promise to give you all the hard-and-fast rules for the business, what will this book teach you? Well, some things are fairly standard across the industry, and you need a good handle on those things when you're starting out. In this book, you'll learn those basics, along with the responsibilities of the entry-level member of the production accounting department – called the clerk – for a $1.8 million independent feature film where the show is SAG-AFTRA and the crew is non-union.

Although we'll be focusing on the world of independent productions, I've left you a few little notes here and there on how the studio system works as well.

We will also briefly discuss payroll service companies, accounting software, and how to network in the accounting industry. Finally, I'll run you through the positions you'll move on to after your time as a clerk, which include second assistant, payroll assistant, payroll coordinator, first assistant, and key accountant. These jobs require more experience, and as you work and learn, you will move up through the ranks. Just like I did.

The most important thing you'll have to do to work in production accounting? READ, READ, READ! *And reading this is a very good start.* You must also ALWAYS pay attention, anticipate what's coming next, and above all, use common sense. This job is not for the lazy or the uncommitted. A short attention span makes for a short career. You must take pride in your own initiative and be prepared to seek out the answers you need.

This book is not just for people looking to enter the field of production accounting. Anyone interested in line producing, production management, production coordinating, or even assistant directing can learn a great deal from these pages. Accounting is a good place to start, because it lays the groundwork for one of the responsibilities all these jobs share: paperwork. (Dun-dun-DUUUUUNNNNN! But actually, you'll soon see how satisfying and even enjoyable production paperwork can be.) Knowledge is power, and my hope is that this book can make you better at your job, more desirable, and more in demand for the production accountants or producers looking to hire.

Sound like the kind of book you need? Great! Here's to becoming a human sponge. Soak up as much as you can. I hope you enjoy.

Table of Contents

Chapter I

Showbiz Shows
(*Film, TV, Reality, Talk Shows, Etc.*)

There are many different types of show in production. Each has different needs and places different demands on the accounting team. The type of show you're working on will affect what is expected of you on your first job, so let's take a quick look at the possibilities.

Studio/Independent Feature Films

On most shows with a budget under $1.8 million, there is a lead account-ant and, if you are really lucky, a person covering several of the other major jobs in the accounting office, namely payroll, accounts payable, and petty cash (don't worry, I'll walk you through what all of those are soon). This type of film is usually SAG-AFTRA (Screen Actors Guild–Ameri-can Federation of Television and Radio Artists – often abbreviated to "SAG") for the actors and non-union for the crew.

Independent features can run as low as $700,000 (*yes, I'm sure there are even $20,000 films out there*) up to blockbusters costing hundreds of millions.

On the really big features, the accounting department can be as many as ten or fifteen people.

Example of the Team:

Financial controller
Production accountant
First assistant accountant
Payroll coordinator – crew
SAG-AFTRA payroll coordinator
Extras payroll coordinator
Petty cash coordinator
P-card coordinator
Second assistant – 2
Clerk – 2
Construction accountant
Masseuse (*I tease, but wow, that would be sweet*)

If there are multiple locations, then there might be different crew members at each location so they can tag-team.

Scripted TV Shows

Personally, I think these jobs are the way to go. Studio scripted shows can have a three- to four-person department, sometimes bigger.

A half-hour scripted show generally has a three- to four-person team once it's been picked up, meaning the studio has decided to take the pilot to series.

A one-hour scripted show can have a five- to six-person team – again, once picked up.

All of these shows will be either full union or **non-affiliate**. A non-affiliate show gives non-union production accountants and assistant accountants most of the same benefits they would find on a union project (see glossary).

Pilots have less manpower in the accounting department because production tends to be short and fast. Pilot season, when the bulk of pilots are made, has traditionally run from late February to mid-April for the studios. (At time of writing, it's unclear how this may change due to COVID-19.)

Location shows can also be huge, depending on the premise of the show, the budget, whether there are multiple locations, and the shooting schedule. A fun side note: while on a distant location, some productions will give the department heads their own cars. They also offer a daily allowance for employees to cover living expenses (called **per diem**), housing, and airfare, as well as shuttles to and from work.

Six-day work weeks are the norm on location, so be prepared. *What, you wanted a life? Silly you.*

A warning, and I cannot overstate this: you must enjoy being away for long periods. This job consumes your personal time, especially if you're new to the field.

Reality and Reality Competition TV Shows

These can be fun since most of these shows are unscripted and you're dealing with everyday people. And let's be honest, most people who appear on reality TV shows do not care at all how they come across.

The accounting department for reality TV usually ranges from three to four people but sometimes has more. Again, it all depends on the budget for the show. These projects can be non-union or union; I normally go for the union shows since you work like a beast on reality TV, and if you're going to be working like a beast, you might as well get all the bells and whistles that a union or non-affiliate show gives to its freelancers. We're talking a medical and dental package, that kind of thing.

A half-hour show is usually a three- to four-person team.

A one-hour show is usually a four- to five-person team.

FYI: I personally have never worked on a pilot for a reality show since they require so much filming time before they have enough footage to slice a pilot together. It's my guess that reality pilots are not worth doing, financially.

Documentaries, Commercials, and Music Videos

The accounting department for these types of show is usually in-house (a staff job), so as a freelancer you're unlikely to be working on them.

Chapter 2

Getting Down to Business

Now that you have an idea of the different types of show you might find yourself working on, let's sketch out the basics of what production accounting involves.

On each show, we work with A/P, payroll for the cast, crew, and extras, petty cash, P-cards, POs, journals, and filing.

Bigger shows will also include A/R, bill backs, integrations, credit cards, cachet cards, multiple locations, set codes, and incentives (if the state has these in place). The list can go on and on...

Yup — just like any specialized field, production accounting is heavy on the acronyms and jargon. But don't worry, you'll get the hang of it all more quickly than you think. Below is a little information on each of the main things you will be doing in the accounting office on any project.

Accounts Payable (A/P)

This is money production owes to outside companies; the term is often used as a shorthand for paying invoices. It's basically paying your bills on steroids. A/P is a big part of the job, so be prepared to do a little research to understand it in depth.

Petty Cash

You really need to have a diligent eye on this puppy. No one else should have access to your PC float if you're the PC custodian. *If you hold the cash, you are the custodian.* Seriously, I can't stress this one enough. This won't be your responsibility on your first job, so pay attention to what the first assistant accountant is doing to learn the ropes.

P-cards or Cachet Cards

These are purchase cards that payroll companies or third-party companies issue. The first assistant advances the card custodian (who is usually the PC custodian), who then floats or sets limits for the cardholders once they turn in their P-cards or **PC envelopes**, which contain a breakdown of all the petty cash receipts for the week. These are mostly used on independent shows. Most studios won't allow P-cards, which are issued by the payroll company, but will work with cachet cards, which are issued by an outside credit card company. All of the studios have manuals that contain all their do's and don'ts, which they will have you read prior to starting. You will be asked to sign a form stating that you have read and understand the manual.

The PC custodian should do a daily tracking of the petty cash, for their own good. The first assistant usually sends an email reminder to the crew on Tuesday morning that PC envelopes are due Wednesday morning for a twenty-four-hour turnaround, due to the approvals needed across the board before you can refloat their cards or cash after the line producer (LP) or production manager (PM) approves.

Beware of the person who doesn't turn in their envelope when they are supposed to. For me, it's a red flag if it's been more than two weeks and someone hasn't turned in anything. And please make sure you tell the LP or PM that the person in question has not turned in their PC envelope. (*Put it in writing.*) The exception is wardrobe, since they have show-and-tell with the director that can delay the PC process.

Unfortunately, this is one area where fraud happens. People buy stuff that wasn't approved or run personal purchases through their PC. Most studios have a strict policy: no receipts can be turned in after thirty days.

Purchase Orders (POs)

These are the forms authorizing the purchase or rental of each item or service the production needs. When a department needs something, it issues a purchase order for that item saying how much it will cost, who will be supplying it, and when the item needs to be paid for. This way, accounting can anticipate the costs coming in for each department and plan accordingly. POs are also essential later in the process for making sure suppliers get paid exactly what they're owed, and if an order has arrived with more or less inventory than expected, this is clearly tracked. If a department has bought or rented something, the PO is to be turned in by end of day by the head of the department that ordered the items, or the department coordinator, with a W-9 (see page 88).

There is no reason to ever turn in a PO if you have the invoice. So many people don't get this.

THE PO IS FOR ANTICIPATING COSTS, AND IF THE INVOICE IS TURNED IN AT THE SAME TIME AS THE PO, ARE YOU ANTICIPATING? NO.

Journals

These are usually for funding and coding correction entries and usually done by either the production accountant, first assistant, or payroll coordinator, depending on how the accountant likes to run things. Journals can also include things like studio bill backs to the show, which won't be your responsibility until much later.

Payroll

This can be either union or non-union, depending on the project. It will usually consist of crew, cast, and extras.

Filing

Everybody's favorite thing (well, it's *my* favorite thing). This is never-ending and everybody has to do it. It's vital for a smooth-running accounting office.

We'll get into detail on some of these things later. For now, make sure you've got your head around these basic terms. They're about to become a huge part of your life.

Chapter 3

Accountants and Payroll and Clerks, Oh My!

As I've mentioned, nothing is truly standard in production accounting; every project is different, every type of show has its own demands, and every accountant has her own way of running her department. Still, over many years of experience, I've picked up most of the tricks of the trade, and I can tell you roughly what to expect. The following is a rundown of the responsibilities of the accounting department, broken down by member of the team. Remember, this is based on how I do my shows and assumes we're looking at a $1.8 million independent feature film, with SAG-AFTRA contracts for the actors and a non-union crew.

Once you do a show all the way through, I recommend you pick this book up again and reread. Some of the concepts might feel a little slippery until you've actually put in some hours in an office, but you'll understand everything much more clearly the second time through and pick up lots of details you may miss on the first pass.

Production Accountant

WHAT THE PRODUCTION ACCOUNTANT DOES:
Hires the team. Be aware, sometimes it takes several hires before they find ex-

actly who they need. Still, it's easier than, say, finding a perfect match on Tinder.

Manages cash flow/funding. Independent projects require a **cash flow** — a spreadsheet detailing the production budget by week — which takes some time to organize. Production accountants might create their own Excel sheet with formulas or buy the Showbiz Cash Flows software from Media Services (we'll talk about the different software options for production accounting soon!). I myself have never used this software — for years, I have used my own Excel sheet, complete with formulas I set up. When you eventually become a production accountant, if you are good with Excel, you too can make your own spreadsheet; otherwise, the Showbiz software can save you the step.

Creates funding requests. On an independent show, once the production accountant has done the cash flow, they do a summary for each week, which becomes the funding request, the formal request for the money to meet all the demands of the budget. It may need adjusting as the show goes on. On a studio project, the accountant won't usually deal with this, at least not in my experience. Studios use "positive pay," which is an option in the accounting software that lets the studio know exactly how much money to transfer to the production for a given check run so the checks can clear.

A production accountant on an independent show will need to be excellent at anticipating which vendor is going to want a huge deposit up front, so they are not short when they need to start writing checks.

Gets contracts to the lead cast. Production accountants are also responsible for getting the lead cast contracts and making sure they get paid. They should always double-check this with Business Affairs — it may not be their responsibility on a given show.

Tracks costs and keeps the LP or PM informed. The accountant keeps track of all costs and makes sure the LP or PM hears about everything that is going on, especially any funny stuff that happens money-wise. They are responsible for approving everything that goes through their department. The accountant starts the process by double-checking the items that were turned in to them for approval. That means making sure each cost or labor item is listed with the correct account code, which tells the accountant where to put each item in the budget, and checking that the **estimate to complete** column (ETC) has enough money to cover all the items they are reviewing. The ETC is a column on the cost report that tells you the balance available to spend to date for each account code. Once the accountant signs off on these things, the approval folder then goes to the LP or PM for final approval. I know, there's quite a lot of jargon in there. But hopefully you're starting to get the hang of it, and by the time you become an accountant, all of this will fit like a puzzle and make perfect sense.

Does reports. I did warn you there would be paperwork. Reports vary from production company to production company. The most basic are **cost report** (CR) packets, which are reviewed by the production accountant and the LP or PM. The review usually takes place on Thursday or Friday, and then the CR is published by end of day Friday or first thing Monday morning.

A CR PACKET INCLUDES:
• CR
• CR cover
• Trial balance
• Current period transaction report
• Bible
• Purchase order report
• Current check register

Alongside the CR packet, bigger studios also require a **hot cost** — a daily summary of overages and underages — variance reports, and sometimes other things. We won't go into those items here, because they're a way in your future if you're just starting out, but you'll learn about them eventually!

PRO TIP: There is a hot cost program built into the Showbiz Timecards software. If your payroll coordinator is using the software and entering everyone's time into the Showbiz Timecards system, you can use this program to save time and energy — but do make sure it is set up. Never assume these things.

Reviews other reports and costs. Production accountants are also responsible for reviewing:
• Any special reports
• **Integration costs** — associated with product placement — this happens on really big shows, primarily reality shows (example: all the Dunkin' Donuts promotion on *America's Got Talent*)
• Insurance claim costs, whether property or **workers' compensation** — filed when someone is hurt on set
• **Bill backs** — costs that the production will bill back to the studio or vice versa. Let's say the show incurs a cost that wasn't budgeted for or an actor asks for something and says he will pay the show back. Those items get their own codes and invoices to make sure the production is reimbursed.

Finally, and most importantly, production accountants are responsible for putting fires out. Not actual fires, of course. *That is not in the job description.*

First Assistant Accountant

This position really prepares you for becoming a production accountant. However, I strongly believe you should have payroll experience behind you as well before moving up to the top spot.

Responsibilities:
- Double-checking the W-9s that have been entered to make sure they are properly coded and marked for 1099s in the accounting system – SO IMPORTANT!!! (See page 88.)
- Auditing both the assistant's work and their own
- Preparing **credit one-sheets** – used for opening vendor accounts
- POs, from beginning to end, unless there is a second assistant accountant
- A/P, from beginning to end, unless there is a second assistant accountant
- Doing **bank reconciles** – balancing the production's check book
- Creating, entering, and posting journals
- Compiling year-end to date 1099 report at the end of the show
- Finalizing insurance claims and giving them to the accountant
- Filing their own paperwork. Yes, I said that.

In addition to all of the above, they are also responsible for making sure the team is doing what they are supposed to be doing.

Another first assistant job is creating summaries for the PC and/or P-card envelopes on the envelope covers. There is a sample PC cover among the forms I've included in the second half of the book. (See page 189.)

They are also responsible for entering the envelopes in the software and double-checking their work, then submitting their PC envelopes with the audit reports to the accountant for review, to ensure the reports attached are in account and entry order for final approval.

Similarly, they enter all A/P and submit invoices with the A/P audit reports to the accountant in account and entry order for final approval. Once that's done, they post, print, and assemble checks with invoices in the order they appear in on the check stub. Next, they submit these to the accountant so that they can sign the checks, along with whoever is the second signature on the checks (usually the LP, PM, studio producer, or production finance executive (PFE)).

Studios generally put a money cap on the production team signing checks — once a check is for more than a certain amount of money, the studio requires that one of their own people countersign it. In my experience, the cap tends to be $50,000 to $100,000. Payroll company checks are the only exception.

And most importantly: filing. Yes, I said filing. Friday is filing day. I find filing to be therapeutic and I really insist on my assistants doing their own, for their own sake. It means they stay organized. *And then, I might smile at them. Maybe.*

The first assistant's final job when the show wraps is to call all the vendors to make sure there is nothing outstanding.

All these duties do not make them the boss — they are still training for the next step — but they are the eyes and ears of the production accountant if they are not in the same office.

Payroll Coordinator

The payroll coordinator (or payroll accountant) is responsible for — you guessed it — all things payroll. The preferred work schedule for this position is Sunday through Thursday. This way they can have everything to the payroll company by Monday. Here are some details on their weekly duties:

Start paperwork. This is, naturally, the paperwork that officially starts each employee's time on the production. The payroll coordinator doesn't have to do the first round of the start paperwork if there is either a second assistant or a clerk on board. I like for these entry-level department members to do this so they understand how important this paperwork is and how to do it correctly, but it goes to the payroll coordinator next. Then the payroll coordinator begins breaking down the paperwork by inserting the coding and anything else that needs to be completed. They are responsible for making sure all the start paperwork is properly filled out and ready to be sent to the payroll company. If the production accountant agrees, the payroll coordinator can also show the clerk how to check the incoming paperwork, so the clerk can take care of that job before the paperwork lands on the payroll coordinator's desk.

Time cards. Being responsible for all payroll means handling the time cards for staff, crew, actors, and extras (although extras turn in vouchers, not time cards). This is a big job, so on particularly large projects, the payroll coordinator may have an assistant to help with it; if they don't have one, I let the clerk help by doing the time cards for the staff, PAs, and extras. After collecting the time cards, the coordinator enters them into whatever time card software the production is using. If software isn't available to them, they will have to go through the cards and calculate each employee's pay, called breaking down the time cards, by hand – something they should know how to do by the time they reach this position. After the time cards are broken down and approved, the payroll coordinator organizes them and then sends them to the payroll company for processing.

Working on a union show involves a lot of variables and details – different tiers and unions, differences between the East and West Coasts, Green Book vs. basic agreements, and so on. If the show is union, the accountant has to send the contract for the show to the head of labor relations at the payroll company so the show can be set up correctly. The legal department or Business Affairs at the studio or production company usually handles this. When the contract is signed, it is given to accounting so we know what concession we pay, and then we forward it to the payroll company.

When you start out as payroll coordinator, DO NOT TAKE A UNION SHOW. Begin on a small non-union show and get your mind around the systems first. This is why I let the clerk do the extras' vouchers and staff's time cards: to get an idea of which parts of accounting appeal to them and which don't. The payroll position can be very overwhelming. *And we don't want you popping Xanax.*

I wish I could say that payroll coordinators don't have hard days, but it's likely they'll have to deal with one or two crew members who just want to be rude. If it happens more than once, the coordinator should let the accountant and the LP know.

It's a good idea for the payroll coordinator to set up a separate email just for all payroll items, which should be recognizable as the payroll email address. For example, the coordinator might format the address like this: **Showname:PYRL@gmail.com.**

TOOLS OF THE PAYROLL TRADE

The payroll coordinator uses a calculator (A LOT), the EP *Paymaster* book, and the Showbiz Timecards software (not required, but certainly helpful).

Along with these tools, they see and use an assortment of paperwork forms on a regular basis:
• All the payroll forms (start forms, I-9s, W-9s, etc.)
• **Deal memos** – contracts that define the employees' rates of pay
• **Call sheets** – daily schedules for the production
• **Daily production reports** – summarizing what occurred on a given day of production
• **Exhibit Gs** – used to write out actors' time cards (they do not write their own)

One type of paperwork the production coordinator starts and the payroll coordinator finalizes deserves a special mention: workers' compensation (WC). If an incident occurs, such as an injury on set, the payroll coordinator is responsible for ensuring all WC paperwork is collected by the production coordinator. The paperwork is then submitted to the workers' compensation department at the payroll company. To keep on top of this part of the job, the payroll coordinator reads the notes section of the daily production reports to see if any injuries have happened on set. It's their responsibility to make sure all the relevant people have all the information they need, including the payroll company and the injured party, and to ensure the production team has all the necessary forms related to on-set injuries prior to shooting.

The payroll coordinator also maintains an Excel payroll cheat sheet for all crew and cast info. See Chapter 17: Production Form Examples for a sample of a payroll cheat sheet (page 191).

At the end of the week, they inform the clerk of anything pending or important to know for Friday. The clerk is the payroll coordinator's liaison on Fridays for any issues.

And lastly, in addition to all these duties, the payroll coordinator helps train the clerk.

(More detail about what the payroll coordinator does awaits you in Chapter 14.)

Second Assistant Accountant

Once someone has tested the waters with clerk duties, the next step is to become a second assistant accountant, usually on a show with a bigger budget. Here they have more responsibilities, such as:

• Preparing the credit applications to open store or vendor accounts
• Double-checking all incoming POs, W-9s, and A/P invoices
• Matching, coding, and prepping all these items for approval
• Entering POs, making copies of the backups, attaching to different PO

colors, and distributing
• Then, of course, filing

They help out in other areas as well, if time allows. When I work with a second assistant on three shows in a row, I have them and the first assistant trade responsibilities on the third show; that way, the second assistant is exposed to a variety of elements of the job.

Clerk

And finally, we've come to the duties of the clerk. This is where you will start out, as many of us did. *And most of us survived.*

From day one, you will be an important member of the team. You'll begin by helping get the office or offices set up. This includes things like checking that the phones are working – and that they can both make and receive calls! – and making sure the printers are behaving. Remember to test everything! Tech has a funny way of mucking things up.

You'll make and post a sign in the accounting office with the show name, company name, mailing address, phone number, and Wi-Fi password, along with the emails for the first assistant and the payroll coordinator.

Then, you'll make a sign for each member of the team: the first assistant, payroll coordinator, and clerk (that's you!). Tape these signs to the most visible side of their desks.

EXAMPLE:
PAYROLL COORDINATOR
BIANCA STEVENS

Ask the first assistant and payroll coordinator if anything else is needed.

(See more about setting up the office in Chapter 6.)

When production is shooting, everyone will be fed by the caterers when they call lunch. You can find the time for the lunch call on the call sheet; it will usually be six hours after the crew is called in the morning. If it is a location show, have the office PA pick up lunch for the office.

If it's not a studio job, organizing lunch will usually be your responsibility, and there will be an amount budgeted for it that you cannot exceed. So be sure to ask either the first or the payroll coordinator what that amount is (and whether money is even available for lunch on your show).

In general, you'll be working with the first and the payroll coordinator. Your questions should be directed to them. All payroll questions go to the payroll coordinator and the rest go to the first.

As you may already be able to tell, there are many different tasks you'll be responsible for. Here are some more of the duties you can expect to have in the office:
• Filing
• Copying
• Research
• Breaking down extras' vouchers and staff and PAs' time sheets, both union and non-union
• Handling all staff and production assistants' paperwork
• Writing the wrap memo and assisting with wrapping out the office — i.e., breaking things down when the show ends

If there's a second assistant accountant on the show, they will do the following tasks — but if there isn't, it's all you, baby! *(Lucky you!)*

• Opening all mail, stamping, and matching POs to invoices, whether mailed or emailed (the PO must be entered into the accounting software prior to receiving the invoice)

• POs (including tracking any voided and filed-out POs and returning any blank ones)

• Entering W-9s

A lot of what we've covered in this chapter won't be relevant for you until years from now. But it never hurts to have a primer on where you're going and what to look out for when you hang up your "clerk" sign on your first desk.

Chapter 4

Software and Payroll Companies

Now that you know what everyone does, let's take a look at how the team does it. You've probably already gathered that working with accounting software and with payroll companies will be a big part of the job. Different accounting teams use different software and payroll companies in their offices. These decisions are usually made by the accountant for independent shows and by a studio person for studio projects, though the studio will give the accountant two or three choices.

Before we go into the details of the options, I want to introduce you to an important member of your team: the paymaster. This may sound like the villain in a Marvel movie, but this is the person you will be working with at your payroll company to process your payroll. *So be very nice to her.* And remember, she is there to help you, but she is only as good as the information you provide her.

Paymasters are juggling many shows at once. If you are messy and disorganized, it makes their job much harder, which means it can take longer to get your payroll turned around. It could mean the cast and crew don't get paid on time. This is bad. It's the kind of thing that forces you to go incognito, unless you want to face the wrath of the best boy grip and gaffer. The easier you make it for your paymaster, the better for you in the end.

Paymasters at these companies are usually on a four-day or five-day work week. I personally like my paymaster to work Monday through Thursday.

All payroll companies process all types of payroll, including union and non-union crew and talent for features, scripted TV, reality TV, commercials, and so on. They all provide tutorials on their websites for their software. I **STRONGLY** recommend watching all available tutorials for any payroll company you are about to work with.

In alphabetical order, here are the most used payroll companies and the software they offer:

CAPS
http://capspayroll.com
CAPS has offices in Los Angeles and New York. Their accounting software is also called CAPS.

CAPS has now been sold to Cast & Crew.

CAST & CREW ENTERTAINMENT
http://www.castandcrew.com
Cast & Crew have several locations throughout the United States, Canada, and the UK. Their accounting software is called PSL. Personally, I prefer PSL to CAPS, because it has more bells and whistles and CAPS can be a bit vague in its presentation.

ENTERTAINMENT PARTNERS
http://www.ep.com/home
Commonly known as EP. They have locations throughout the United States, with affiliates in Canada, the UK, Asia, and Puerto Rico.

EP offers multiple options for accounting software: Classic Vista, Vista Exchange, Vista 5, and SmartAccounting (formerly known as Ease Payroll). They also offer two new potentially helpful types of software for start card and time card entry, called SmartStart and SmartTime, respectively. More info about both can be found on their website.

Lastly, EP sells a book, *The Paymaster*. Updated every year, this is a highly recommended tool that helps you with the guidelines of paying different union crew, members of SAG-AFTRA, DGA (Directors Guild of America), WGA (Writers Guild of America), extras, etc.

MEDIA SERVICES
www.mediaservices.com
And their software:
www.mediaservices.com/showbiz

Media Services, now owned by Cast & Crew, has offices in Los Angeles, New York, and Louisiana. Their web-based accounting system is called MediaWeb.

This one is high on my list of favorites because their Software Support department is insanely efficient and their software is very easy to navigate — both huge pluses. They also have an online store selling production software goodies, not to mention a lot of super helpful tutorials on their website.

To top it off, Media Services offers the free *Showbiz Labor Guide*:
www.mediaservices.com/showbiz-software/showbiz-labor-guide

I know, I've just given you a bunch of research to do. But if you're willing to take the time and educate yourself on all of the different payroll websites, you will find a lot of information available that will help you on your first job.

All these companies provide technical support both during the day and after hours. Just be prepared for a long wait time when dealing with the bigger payroll companies.

But these help lines are only helpful if you know what you're talking about. Most of the tech support peeps are not familiar with accounting terms or processes. They are tech support, not accounting support. So be sure to put in your hours on YouTube and the Internet in general to view as many basic accounting videos as possible. Especially if you have no formal schooling in accounting.

There's something else you should keep in mind: payroll companies require a deposit from the production company, especially if it's an independent company, before they will process payroll. Sometimes it can be hefty. Toward the middle of the show, they may let you draw down against the deposit. You'll have to ask. Their answer will be contingent on how many weeks are left of production and how many times you have worked with them in the past.

HELPFUL TIP:

All of the payroll companies offer free software training and have marketing departments that you can send your resume to, as well as places on their websites where you can upload your resume for people looking for crew.

Use them.

Budgeting

There's one essential aspect of production accounting that isn't covered by the accounting software we've looked at so far – budgeting. When you think about the amounts of money involved in any show and the number of different elements in play, you'll see why the accountant would want some electronic help with this!

The budget program most productions use is called Movie Magic Budgeting. This has been around a long time and it has lots of bells and whistles.

So, really take your time and learn every nook and cranny of it.

You won't be using MMB until you become a production accountant, but don't wait until then to learn. There really is a lot the program can do.

The budget of an independent show is done by the producer, though sometimes they hire an LP or PM for the job. It is usually very detailed and tells the financial story of the script. The software has different templates for most studios, which help the user create what they need. To get a sense of what a full budget for a show looks like in this software, see the sample beginning on page 158.

You can only purchase MMB from EP; they are based in Burbank, CA.

Media Services has a budgeting program as well. Of course, which program you choose to use all comes down to personal preference.

Chapter 5

Tools of the Trade

Knowledge and skill can only take you so far. For every job, you will need tools to assist you. Here are the tools of the trade for an independent feature film with a $1.8 million budget. On studio shows, the studio provides equipment for accounting, but if your show is independent, you're on your own.

For starters, you will need a notepad. Simple, yet vital. You'll need to take notes each time you are asked to do something, anytime you learn something new, and whenever you are called into a meeting.

Next, the two most important tools in every accounting office: a safe and a ten-key calculator. This is not like the calculators you used in school or the one on your smartphone. Please do not use the calculator on your phone. Trust me. If using a ten-key calculator confuses you at first, YouTube has several excellent tutorial videos. (*Ah, good old YouTube!*)

Now on to the tech stuff. Laptop or desktop computer. ("Duh, I know!") This is, of course, an essential tool for accessing all your software (and your tutorials!) and more. You will also need a scanner. This is the primary way you'll get all your paperwork to the payroll company, which is important, especially if you are a small show.

If you're using a Mac, make sure the software you've chosen is compatible; some of them were designed solely for PCs.

Lastly for tech stuff, a printer. You'll either need one for each person or a large copier with scanning abilities, **for accounting only to use**, and then also a printer for the first assistant and payroll coordinator to print all the checks on check-run day.

You will need toners for each printer (or possibly ink – though with the cost of ink and the amount you will print, go with toner printers). The most important toner is the **MICR**, the special toner used to print checks. See your first assistant to help you with the vendor source.

Moving on from tech, you'll want some miscellaneous useful tools. To help you stay organized, get some premade stamps. You can find the main ones at any office supply store, but you'll need to get some custom-made – order these from the store's printing department.

Here are the stamps you will need:
• Approval
• Entered
• Scanned
• Posted
• Date and Time (*optional*)

You'll use these on invoices, PC envelopes, payroll, and journals.

While you're at the office supply store, be sure to pick up these other important items:
• Ruler
• Post-it notes
• Pens/pencils
• Twizzlers (*not necessary, but delicious*)

Get anything that will help you with the job and help you stay organized. I can't stress enough how important it is to stay organized. Have I mentioned yet that this job involves *filing?* You're still at the supply store, right? Grab these helpful things too:

1/3-cut file folders and Avery 1/3-cut file folder labels. These come in a range of colors, which you can use to file different categories of paperwork. For example, here are the colors I use and how I use them:

WHITE LABELS: All general items (separated into A/P reports, bank reconcile reports, checks, POs, journals, payroll reports, petty cash reports, etc.). Basically, these folders are for items with no money value. I also file all pink copies of POs here, in numerical order.

The labels include the name of the item – the item category – the name of the company – the city you shot in – the year.

EXAMPLES:

BANK RECONCILES		GNL
ACCOUNTING PROD. LLC	NY	2020

YELLOW LABELS: I file all cast paperwork (one file folder for each cast member) and extras by union status and W/E (week ending date).

EXAMPLES: (2 SEPARATE LABELS)

UNION EXTRAS W/E 01212020		PYRL
ACCOUNTING PROD. LLC	NY	2020

NON-UNION EXTRAS W/E 01212020		PYRL
ACCOUNTING PROD. LLC	NY	2020

BLUE LABELS: All staff payroll. The check copy is stapled on top of the time card, and if there is a box rental form or a mileage form, it gets stapled behind the time card. Staff deal memos and any other paperwork are also filed here. Names are always filed as:

LAST NAME/FIRST NAME   **PYRL**
ACCOUNTING PROD. LLC   **NY**   **2020**

RED LABELS: All accounts payable.

MACY'S   **A/P**
ACCOUNTING PROD. LLC   **NY**   **2020**

GREEN LABELS: PC and P-cards. File under the employee's name. Again, you'll write that as LAST NAME/FIRST NAME.

STEVENS/BIANCA   **P/C**
ACCOUNTING PROD. LLC   **NY**   **2020**

Know your placements for your labels!

The 1/3-cut file folders give you a left, middle, and right tab, which you should set up like this (see next page for tab positions):

A	B	C
D	E	F
G	H	I
J	K	L
M	N	O
P	Q	R
S	T	U
V	W	X
Y	Z	

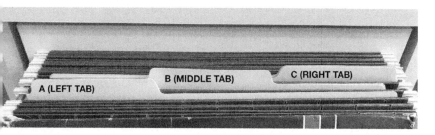

Image 1: 1/3-cut file folders

Now you know your ABCs, tell me, where does STEVENS/BIANCA fall on the tabs? Left, middle, or right?

If you said left, filing will not be a problem for you. Any vendor whose last name or company name begins with a letter on the left-hand side gets a left tab, one starting with a letter in the middle gets a middle tab, etc.

When you become a payroll coordinator, you will need some other special tools:

• EP's *Paymaster* book for the current year (if your show is a union show)

EP's *Paymaster* is available for purchase through their website, and a new edition is released each year with updates for all the unions. Most of the ways to pay stay the same; it's the scale rates (the baseline union rates) that change.

• Showbiz Timecards Bundle, available through Media Services. This is a one-time purchase and then you pay for updates. (If you use MediaWeb, they let you use the Showbiz software for free.)

Now that we've covered all the tools in the office, it's time to go over the many paper items you will need. And let me tell you, accounting is paper-centric. (*Sorry, trees.*) FYI, some of the payroll companies are really working on going automated.

Forms Provided by the Payroll Company

The payroll company provides you with the following forms, and you'll ultimately return them to the payroll company after they're filled out.

NON-UNION START FORMS

NON-UNION LOAN-OUT START FORMS

UNION CREW/CAST START FORMS

UNION LOAN-OUT CREW/CAST START FORMS

W-4

NON-UNION EXTRA VOUCHERS

UNION EXTRA VOUCHERS:
Ask the payroll coordinator on your show how many extras are in the budget, and order that quantity of vouchers and a few spare.

I-9 FORMS:
You can also get these from the IRS website, just in case you need any additional copies or a digital version.

BRICKS OF BLANK PAYROLL CHECKS (if the show is on remote check printing; most are these days)

Find out from the payroll coordinator the size of the crew, the number of extras, and the SAG-AFTRA cast. That's how many checks you should ask for from the payroll company. The standard number of checks per ream used to be 500, but always double-check with the payroll company how many are in the ream they are giving you.

Double the check quantity and request boxes of envelopes for that number. Again, ask how many come in a box.

They may only give you one copy of each of the following forms – you'll have to keep making copies throughout the show.

CWTPA (California Wage Theft Prevention Act of 2011)

BOX RENTAL FORM (both invoice and inventory)

MILEAGE FORM

Supplies from Form Consultants

1-800-719-6817
Lew.formconsultants@gmail.com

A/P BLANK CHECK STOCK
Ask the first assistant how many they will need, since they are the one in charge of A/P check runs.

POs
Order your POs, if they are four-part, from the vendor Form Consultants; they are our usual go-to for this. If the PO is electronic, see the production coordinator or ask your first assistant if they have the template. Then create a PO log and assign numbers to the department heads. (See the sample PO log in Chapter 10, page 79.)

Stay on top of all of your forms and your check stock and make sure you NEVER RUN OUT!

Just a typical day in the accounting office

Chapter 6

Get Ready, Get Set...

Now you have the basics down, it's time to set up the office.

The person responsible for getting the items the production accounting team needs for the office is the production office coordinator, or POC; on a non-union show, this person's title is production coordinator, or PC. These items include spare keys to the door, desks, chairs, a shredder, startup office supplies, file cabinets, phones, Internet, a safe, and anything else you may need, such as, for example, the form to get you a parking space.

Once the items come in, it's your responsibility as the clerk to organize the room the way the accountant wants it, and from then on submit supply orders to the coordinator. Or, if that seems like a lot of trouble to go to for some staplers and toner, you can get a small PC float and acquire your own supplies (*which is the way I like to go, hence your shopping list in Chapter 5*).

I usually have the clerk start early, if I get a clerk in the budget; otherwise, I have the first assistant set up.

On the desks, there should be an inbox for each person in the department. Once each team member starts, they can set up their own desk how they like it.

Just inside the office door, set up a six-foot folding table if space allows (smaller if it doesn't) for inboxes — bins where the crew submits paperwork throughout the day, organized by category.

I like to organize the inboxes on this table like this, starting closest to the door and moving into the room:
1) Mail
2) A/P and POs
3) PC and P-cards
4) Payroll (with a sign on the wall asking people to place their documents face down) — no one but the accounting team is allowed to go in and retrieve a crew member's payroll paperwork

Under the table live the surplus supplies:
• Blank POs
• Blank crew paperwork
• Blank cast paperwork
• Blank extra vouchers
• Blank PC covers
• I-9s
• CWTPA
• **Box rental forms** — for when an employee or contractor is renting items of their own to production for use on the show
• **Mileage forms** — for logging miles an employee or contractor has driven on production business
• A case of paper
• Extra printer toners
• Etc.

If space is limited and you can't fit a folding table in the office, then the surplus goes in the file cabinets. Can't fit it there either? Find a secure place and make it work. (*Love Tim Gunn.*) Remember, initiative is part of what you're being paid for!

Blank payroll and A/P check stock live in a file cabinet and are locked up daily.

On top of the file cabinets, there should be empty inboxes to store the to-be-filed items, one inbox for each file cabinet and category. This way, there won't be paperwork all over the room. All items should go in the inboxes face down.

EXAMPLE:
The first file cabinet houses A/P and payroll, so on top of the cabinet should be one inbox for A/P, one for crew payroll, one for cast payroll, and one for extras payroll.

This will help when Thursday or Friday rolls around and filing has to happen, or if you need to find something that hasn't been filed yet.

These are the kinds of details that give you the best shot at a smooth, efficient office, and the more of them you can take care of before you start, the less frustration there will be through the whole run of the production.

Chapter 7

Clerk Work: Payroll, A Love Story

On an independent show, the clerk assists with payroll if time allows. In this chapter, I will go over some of what you will be doing, step by step.

First of all, you'll need to be familiar with all the payroll documents. As of 2020, the forms below are what you will need to process payroll. These forms are all the same across the board. The only things that vary are the payroll company and whether the forms are **non-union or union**.

For a crew member paid as an individual, you will need:
- BLANK DEAL MEMO FORM (the blank master form is usually with the PC/POC, who should have sent the blank deal memo to the production accountant and payroll coordinator; originated by the legal team)
- BLANK START FORM
- NEW W-4 FORM
- BLANK I-9
- BLANK TIME CARD
- BLANK CWTPA (California Wage Theft Prevention Act of 2011; applies to projects shooting in California and those based in California but shooting elsewhere; only needed for non-union crew)
- ACH DIRECT DEPOSIT FORM (if the show is set up to use direct deposit)

For a crew member paid as a **loan-out**, meaning as provided by a corporation – some individual contractors are actually corporations for tax purposes – you will need:

- BLANK DEAL MEMO FORM (again, the master is usually with the PC/POC)
- W-9 (you can get this from the IRS website – only the first page is needed)
- BLANK LOAN-OUT FORM
- BLANK TIME CARD
- BLANK CWTPA
- ACH DIRECT DEPOSIT FORM (if the show is set up to use direct deposit)

All these forms, except the deal memo and W-9, come from the payroll company.

A check authorization form may be included for anyone who wants their check to go to someone other than the payee. You'll need to consult the crew list and/or cast list to see who the payee's manager or agent is and email them for information. And you will definitely want to stay on top of this – people get angry if their checks go to the wrong place, even if they didn't tell you where they should go. *You're a mind-reader now, but you don't get paid extra for that.*

If the employee wants to be paid as a loan-out, the payroll company would prefer the company be a C or an S corporation. If it is an LLC, it will require additional paperwork. *It wouldn't be accounting without adding more bloody paperwork.*

Paying an LLC: If the LLC is owned by a corporation, it will need to provide proof of ownership. If not, it will need to provide the IRS acceptance letter in response to Form 8832 (the most common) showing that the LLC is being treated as a C- or S-corp. This is for tax reporting purposes. In addition, it should have a copy of its articles of organization.

You can sometimes find these on the California Secretary of State website.

Paying a multimember/partnership LLC: You will need the partnership agreement or a redacted 1065 tax return.

If the LLC is unable to collect all of the necessary paperwork, it is considered an individual and must be paid as one. That means the person will have to fill out all the paperwork for an individual (the start paperwork and I-9).

Since you'll be helping the payroll coordinator, your responsibility will be to check all the paperwork that comes in to make sure that all i's are dotted and all t's are crossed. (Note: On a studio show, the production coordinator is responsible for all the start paperwork and for turning it in to the payroll coordinator.)

Each payroll company has its own union and non-union forms, and you'll need to familiarize yourself with the forms your particular company uses. To get you started, I've included samples of the blank start forms from Media Services in Chapter 17.

There are six spots that I would say 95% of crew members miss on the start form. It will be up to you to catch them:

1. Occupation
2. Union/occ code (if applicable)
3. Start date
4. Their rates
5. Signature
6. W-4

The three most common things missing on time cards are:
1. Occupation
2. Signature
3. An attached box rental form – payroll companies now require you to attach one each week or the employee will be taxed on their box rental pay. And it has to be the form provided by the payroll company, not a generic box rental form. This is for legal reasons.

Going back to the start packet, the next thing for you to check is the I-9. The most common problem here? There's always somebody who forgets to attach a backup copy of their ID for the Immigration and Naturalization Services signoff on the second page. You'll need to get ahold of that copy – either they can send it to you or you can ask them to come in and sign off in person, ID in hand. Once the first check is cut and you know you have no issues getting the person paid, you can shred the I-9 and ID backup. For security reasons, I don't advise keeping these around the office, and because the payroll company is the employer of record (the employer for tax purposes), we don't need the I-9s once payroll has them. In my office, the only ones I keep are copies of green cards and paperwork for non-resident aliens authorized to work. (*This is only on independent shows.*)

As all the paperwork comes in, double-check and make sure the items above and everything else are filled out. If you are missing anything, put a Post-it on the relevant form marking what you need, and then email the crew member saying you are missing whatever it is and asking them to come in to see you. You may need to do a lot of these. (You would think they would be diligent in getting their paperwork filled out correctly – that's how they get paid!) Always make sure you cc the payroll coordinator. Their email should be on the employee start form. If it isn't, look on your crew list.

Here's an example of what the subject line of your email should read:
Show name, payroll department, missing item or items, name

Acctg Rocks_pyrl_missing items_B. Stevens

In the body of the email, outline exactly what you are missing. Don't be surprised if you have to babysit. It's part of the job.

Keep a stack of incompletes in a secure area at your desk. MAKE SURE you are checking up on these daily. If an employee doesn't get back to you by the end of the second day, send another email. Still have people you haven't heard from by the fourth day? Give the stack of the remaining incompletes to the production coordinator and let her know you've reached out and heard nothing. If paperwork is incomplete and not submitted to the payroll company, then the employee won't get paid.

Remember to make a list of the start forms you give the production coordinator with the date you gave them to her, and then give the same list to the payroll coordinator. Keeping everyone in the loop is good practice and part of your job from day one.

Once everything is coded with the appropriate account code from the budget and you've double-checked that the rates are on the forms (if they aren't, stick Post-its on them to ask what the rates are), then the completed stacks will get pushed through for approval.

Approvals should happen daily, so be sure to get the good stacks (stacks of paperwork that is complete, with no missing elements or blank fields) organized by department. They should be clearly marked with a highlighter, a "sign here" flag, or an X in a different color pen where the accountant and LP or PM need to sign or answer your Post-it questions. (Make sure you leave enough room on the Post-it for answers.)

You then give the good stack to the payroll coordinator, who will double-check what you are doing. If there are any issues, she will tell you. Make sure you give the payroll coordinator a sheet listing the start forms you are giving her so later you can check whether or not everything was returned to you.

The payroll coordinator will then put the items in the approval folder for signatures from the production accountant and LP or PM.

When the approval folder is returned, check the forms in it against your list and cross off the ones that have now been returned to you. If any items are missing, go back to the payroll coordinator for round two. Double-check to make sure that all signatures are there and all questions have been answered. If the higher-ups missed anything, ask for it again. Tape the Post-it notes with answers on them to the backs of the forms you had questions about. And make sure all four corners are taped down — these will go through the scanner!

On studio shows, the production coordinator takes over all the start paperwork to chase people down for their IDs and to double-check that the crew members have filled everything out correctly.

What You Scan to the Paymaster at the Payroll Company

When the payroll coordinator gives you the go-ahead, you'll send the payroll forms to the paymaster. To find out who your paymaster is, ask your payroll coordinator for their name, phone number, and email. Or you can look on the vendor list, which you can get from the production coordinator.

The only forms that the payroll company ever gets are the ones that have their logo on them. The few exceptions are the I-9s, W-4s, check authorizations, and any DGA or SAG-AFTRA contracts.

NEVER send them deal memos. The payroll company doesn't want them, and you don't want to annoy the payroll company.

(I know, cheesy — but cute!)

Time cards are due at the end of Friday night from the crew. If they are working Saturday, time cards need to be in by Sunday, no later than noon.

There's nothing worse than coming in on a Sunday and finding there's nothing to do but sit there listening to crickets.

Signs should be posted outside of the accounting offices and throughout the area if it's a studio location. *If you're not working in a studio, post on porta-potty doors.* Lots of traffic there. Let people know time cards are due on Friday night and that if they're working Saturday they should email scanned copies of their cards to the email address the payroll coordinator created for the show, which will usually look something like **Showname_yr_pyrl@gmail.com.**

You really shouldn't use your personal email for work emails, because at the end of the show you'll forward the messages to the accountant or whoever at the studio needs them, and it makes that person's life easier if they can tell immediately what those emails are about. It also protects your privacy.

You can also ask the assistant directors (ADs) to post this on the call sheet on Thursdays and Fridays: **"Time cards are due!"**

Submitting Payroll

Once you've broken down your stack of time cards for production staff and production assistants and the vouchers for extras, you'll submit them to the payroll coordinator, who will check your work and make sure everything is correct. And hopefully after the second time you submit, they will see that you know what you're doing and you'll be able to skip this step and go straight to submitting for approvals. But don't get cocky.

HOT TIP: Since you get the extra vouchers daily, I suggest you break them down each day and have them ready to scan on Monday of the following week. Take every opportunity to make your life easier. Things come up and you may not be able to do this every day, but if you can, definitely do.

Next, you'll place the completed time cards in the "approvals for payroll" folder for the accountant to sign off, along with straggler start forms or any other payroll forms needing approval.

Extra vouchers are the only ones the LP doesn't sign off on, and maybe some accountants will let you sign off on them yourself. But I won't! *I told you not to get cocky.*

Once the folder is returned, scan the production staff and PA time cards and name the PDF:

SHOW NAME_WE DATE_PROD. STAFF AND PA'S

Then do two separate scans for the extras, one for non-union forms and one for union forms:

SHOW NAME_WE DATE_NU EXTRAS

SHOW NAME_WE DATE_UNION EXTRAS

After you scan the time cards, straggler start cards, and any other payroll items, email the PDFs to your paymaster at the payroll company, cc'ing your payroll coordinator. (Always make sure everything is approved.) I enforce a Monday 3 p.m. deadline as the ultimate cutoff for the show to receive crew time cards. Anything that comes in after that, I date and time stamp and push until the next week. The exception is new start forms at the beginning of a show, which should be sent daily so that the payroll company can build their database and everyone can be paid on time.

Remember, your paymaster is in the office Monday through Thursday. It can take the paymaster 48 hours to turn around payroll edits for you, so you won't get any until late Wednesday if you've scanned the payroll on Monday. That leaves plenty of time to do other stuff until you get the edits.

When the edits come in, double-check the time cards you broke down against the edits for coding, hourly rate, and final dollar amounts to make sure that they match. If it's the first edit of the production, also check the employee's address, number of dependents, and marital status.

If the edit doesn't have any issues, you can send an email asking the paymaster to release the edit (remember to cc your payroll coordinator, always).

If there are issues, I usually email my paymaster to see when they are available to talk. Please make sure you are prepared, and go through the payroll efficiently and as quickly as possible. I don't recommend just calling them. It's best to schedule a time or you might catch them off-guard while they are working on other shows. They have way more shows than you have, and you do not want to monopolize their time. You can also send a detailed but concise email with exact corrections.

Once edits are released and you receive the final invoices, one of the following will happen:

1) If your show is in town (in Los Angeles) and you are having EP print your payroll checks in their office rather than doing remote check printing, fill out a run slip and give it to the production coordinator. This form authorizes a production assistant to go to the payroll company (called making a run) to pick up the payroll. Make sure the run slip includes a list of the numbers of the invoices that the runner needs to pick up. Please coordinate with your in-house payroll coordinator so you can be efficient with runs. Try not to send the poor runner to the payroll company more than once. Some companies offer complimentary delivery; talk to your paymaster about that option.

2) If you're set up with remote check printing, find out from your in-house payroll coordinator if they want you to wait to print all the cast, crew, and extras payroll checks at once when all the payroll is released and completed or if you can print out just the checks you've been working on at this stage. Then go from there.

Switch the toner in your printer to MICR (remember your list of supplies?), print the checks, and then replace the normal cartridge.

Then it's time to make copies of all the payroll checks and staple them to the time cards, in the following order:

Check copy
Time card
Box rental form (if they have one)
Mileage form (if they have one)

Organize the original checks by department, then stuff the payroll in envelopes, with the relevant department written in the corner of each envelope.

If the show is union, you give out checks on Thursday by lunch; if it's non-union, on Friday.

And voilà! You've gotten everyone paid! *You are now everyone's favorite person.* For about two minutes. (*As Xenia Onatopp once told James Bond, "Enjoy it while it lasts."*)

Chapter 8

Paid, In Full

So you know how to do basic payroll. You're all set to go, right? Well, no. Do you understand how payroll itself works yet? I didn't think so. Let's take a look, so all this paper-pushing has some meaning behind it.

Labor Laws and Pay Hours

Here's a little info on pay hours and the labor laws. This stuff varies by state, so make sure you double-check what the rules are in the place you are working.

The most popular locations for production are California, Georgia, and New York. The below website gives you the minimum wage per state and lets you know how they calculate overtime (OT).

https://www.dol.gov/whd/minwage/america.htm#stateDetails

There are two types of employee: **exempt** and **non-exempt**. Exempt employees have a flat weekly rate and are exempt (see what they did there?) from all OT, meal penalties, etc. Non-exempt employees are paid by the hour. All non-exempt employees must have an hourly wage, and all time cards must reflect their hours worked and meal breaks taken.

Ask your paymaster for a current list of pre-approved exempt job titles. Not just anyone can be paid as exempt. It's usually people like department heads, producers, editors, etc. Anyone who is exempt can write "WORKED" across their time card instead of filling in specific hours.

Keep in mind, this is only for crew. The cast is broken down differently, but you'll learn this once you are a payroll coordinator – if you should choose to do payroll solely. I will also go over SAG-AFTRA cast payroll briefly in Chapter 14.

Calculating Pay Hours

The term *pay hours* doesn't just refer to the number of hours an employee worked and must be paid for. It refers to the number of hours an employee would have had to work at their hourly rate, also called *straight time*, to get to the total amount of pay they are due, including OT. Confused? Here is a quick lesson on how to calculate pay hours.

For the purpose of calculation, we write straight time as 1x – the employee's hourly rate times one.

Let's assume your production is based in California. California law states that anything over eight hours is paid at 1.5x up to the twelfth hour and anything over that is paid at 2x.

Most people on a production are put on a guarantee of either ten- or twelve-hour days. For our example, let's use a daily rate of $300 for a twelve-hour day, five-day week. (FYI, flat rates like this usually only happen on non-union shows.)

To find an employee's hourly rate, you need to figure out their pay per hour based on their guarantee.

All right. Here we go. If the guarantee is twelve hours and the first eight of those are calculated at straight time (1x) and the remaining hours at 1.5x, then that means there are four 1.5x hours.

If you take those four hours and multiply them by 1.5x, you get six. Six plus the eight straight hours equals fourteen pay hours. You with me?

So, if the rate is $300/day for twelve hours, and the employee worked fourteen pay hours... the hourly rate is $21.4285. ALWAYS calculate to the fourth decimal point so that you can get the closest to the penny.

For example, if you take $21.4285 x 14 = $299.999 and round up, you get $300 exactly. If you take $21.42 x 14 you only get $299.88, which is too far from the mark to just round up. Imagine what one could do with those extra twelve cents!

The same goes if you are given a weekly rate that you need to convert to an hourly one. Eight hours a day for five days is forty straight hours. If you have someone making $2,500 a week for sixty hours, that is twenty hours of 1.5x.

20 x 1.5 = 30

Then you add the thirty to the forty straight hours to get seventy weekly pay hours. Divide the total weekly pay by the number of weekly pay hours to find the hourly rate.

$2,500 / 70 = $35.7142

Got it? Easy, right?!

You will use this a lot in payroll, whether the crew is union or non-union.

Non-Union

In this section, you will learn some specific guidelines for non-union payroll in California.

Every state has its own labor laws, which include things like minimum wage and overtime rules. All non-union guidelines follow Wage Order 12, which establishes these guidelines for our industry. You can find this online (https://dir.ca.gov/IWC/IWCArticle12.pdf).

One thing to keep in mind is that the "better provisions prevail." This means that if your production is from California (the only state with meal penalties and 2x OT), then those conditions follow the production even if you are working in another state. The production can also always choose to pay more as long as it is a "better deal."

MINIMUM WAGES
Applicable to employers with twenty-five employees or less
Basic minimum rate (per hour): $11.00
Premium pay after designated hours: More than eight hours: time and a half. More than twelve hours: double time. More than forty hours in the week: time and a half.
Work on the seventh consecutive workday: First eight hours: time and a half. More than eight hours: double time.
Applicable to employers with twenty-six employees or more
Basic minimum rate (per hour): $12.00

For more detail, please google the California Labor Code, section 510.

From 2017 through 2023, the minimum wage will increase annually on a set schedule, and it will be adjusted annually thereafter based on a set formula.

NOTE: The overtime premium rate is one and one half times the employee's regular rate, unless otherwise specified.

Non-union crew pay is one of the easiest to calculate.

Here's what you'll need to make sure you are breaking the time cards correctly.

First, grab all the completed paperwork:
• Crew deal memo – you need this for the first payroll you submit for payment. Get a blank copy from Business Affairs, legal, or your coordinator. Give it to the crew member to fill in, and then get it back. (You may have to chase them.) You'll use the completed and approved deal memos and start forms to create your payroll cheat sheet, which you will keep updating as new completed start forms come in. (See page 191 for a payroll cheat sheet example.)
• Non-union start form, AKA start card (this comes from the payroll company)
• I-9
• W-4
• W-9 if the employee is a loan-out
• Emergency contact sheet
• Check authorization (if applicable)

Each payroll company has a union and non-union side, so make sure you're dealing with the right paperwork – or you'll end up giving out the wrong forms and time cards.

As I briefly mentioned before, there are two types of employee: exempt and non-exempt. Here is some more info on what that means:

NON-EXEMPT EMPLOYEES

By definition, non-exempt employees are not exempt from wage and hour labor laws. This means they are paid by the hour with an hourly rate.

Each non-exempt employee must show accurate in and out times on their time card in order to be paid correctly. They also must mark the start and end times of any meals they took. Time cards always need two signatures before submission: one from the employee confirming their times are correct, and one from a supervisor approving the times.

EXEMPT EMPLOYEES

These are usually department heads; however, your payroll company can provide you with a current list of exempt titles so you know who can write a flat "worked" across their time card.

Exempt employee pay can be based on a five-day work week, with additional pay for the sixth and seventh days worked. This should be written out on the start form.

We've been over pay hours. Here are some other important things you'll need to know to calculate non-union payroll.

CALIFORNIA NON-EXEMPT EMPLOYEES

For the first five consecutive days a non-exempt employee works, they are paid their hourly rate for their first eight hours of the day. That increases to 1.5x straight time after eight hours, then to 2x straight time after twelve hours.

On the employee's sixth day at work in a row, they are paid at 1.5x straight time for their first twelve hours and 2x straight time for anything after that.

If the poor employee has to work seven days in a row, on the seventh day they are paid at 1.5x for the first eight hours and at 2x for anything after that. So maybe that seventh day isn't so bad after all.

Meal penalties: California is the only state that pays meal penalties for non-union crew (union crews always get them, and are paid differently). If a crew member is from California or working in California, they will be eligible. Crew members get a meal penalty if more than six hours go by between the call time and when lunch is called, or more than six hours between the end of lunch and wrap. The penalty is one hour of pay for the day.

These can be avoided by having a **non-deductible break**, an extra meal between the official meals that isn't counted as a break or deducted from the hours worked. It's indicated on the time cards with a simple NDB (B for "break" or "breakfast") or NDD (D for "dinner") added to the morning or evening. Note: There's no need to mark this for exempt crew members. We're not calculating their hours anyway, so it isn't relevant.

RIGHT-TO-WORK LAWS

"Right-to-work" laws are in place to make sure that an employee's initial or continued employment is not affected by their lack of membership in a union, and they do not permit a union to require membership. These laws vary by state.

However, this doesn't mean that a production company can sign an agreement with a union and then just ignore that agreement if they're in a right-to-work state. The company still has to abide by the terms of the agreement for all the employees it would usually cover, whether or not they are in the union. In other words, if your production is based in Florida, a right-to-work state, and you have an agreement with a union, production can hire non-union employees but must treat them and pay them the same way they would treat and pay a union employee.

Please ask your paymaster for an up-to-date list of right-to-work states.

DEDUCTION OF MONEY OWED TO PRODUCTION COMPANY

We never withhold payment from a crew member's check because they owe PC back to the company, unless it is written otherwise on the deal memo and the statement is signed by the crew member. It's illegal. (The only exceptions are federal and state liens and federal and state taxes.)

DIRECT DEPOSIT

Most payroll companies will use direct deposit (DD), and they will ask the production company for a large deposit if there are more than five people on the DD list to make sure the payroll company is not at risk if we don't wire the money to their bank account. Ask your payroll company for the direct deposit form if the payroll coordinator doesn't have it.

PER DIEM, MILEAGE, AND BOX RENTAL

Per diem is issued on a weekly basis on location shows; some offices issue cash, sometimes per diem is put on employees' time cards. This is up to the accountant and LP.

Some of the payroll companies also give us a blank mileage form, which must be filled out correctly or it will be kicked back and the crew member will be taxed. These must be submitted weekly. Check the current federal limit for the mileage rate. If the payroll company doesn't have a rate, just create your own, keeping the federal limit in mind.

Each payroll company has a blank box rental form, and this also needs to be turned in on a weekly basis. Be sure to use the rental form for the payroll company you are working with. This is for legal reasons.

Box rentals can be anything the crew member owns that is being used on the show, such as laptops, printers, cell phones, etc. They must be approved by the LP and PM.

Please note that box rentals are reported on Form 1099 – we'll talk about this and other tax forms soon.

Workers' Comp

When someone is hurt on set, a workers' comp claim needs to be filed. This is above the clerk's paygrade, but I want you to be prepared for a long career in the industry, so pay attention!

The initial paperwork is filled out by the first AD on set, and whoever accompanied the injured crew or cast member then sends it to the production coordinator, who double-checks that everything is correct on the form. They will need to have the paperwork from the medic or the ER to submit it to the WC department at the payroll company, along with the employee's start form.

Once the payroll coordinator has submitted the forms to the payroll company and the original paperwork is turned in to the accounting office for the production accountant to review, the payroll coordinator makes sure that the right people have what they need, and the process is started.

The show payroll coordinator then sends an email to the crew member and cc's the WC contact at the payroll company (THIS WON'T BE YOUR PAYMASTER). They will let the crew member know to whom to send the invoices. There is nothing more frustrating for an injured crew or cast member than being told, "I don't know who the right contact is, let me check."

So, when the payroll coordinator gets word from the WC department at the payroll company, the payroll coordinator should cc via email the injured crew or cast member, production coordinator, and accountant to let them know that all paperwork has been submitted and that the contact is so-and-so at the WC department of the payroll company.

This does not mean that we are no longer involved if the crew member has any issues, though your personal involvement does end when you leave the show. If the claim is large, please be sure to let the legal department of the show know.

RIGHT. Deep breath. You've made it through the payment and labor laws primer. As always, though, keep doing your own research, and make sure you stay on top of any changes.

Chapter 9

Extras! Extras! Read All About Them

As a clerk, you will more than likely be helping with extras payroll. Extras payroll is super easy, and I personally love breaking down the extra vouchers.

Once shooting starts, you'll be receiving various things from the AD department via the production coordinator, including:
• Call sheet
• Extras vouchers with a **skin sheet** – a page of information about that day's extras
• Extras release forms
• Daily production reports (DPRs)
• Exhibit Gs
• Whatever else the production coordinator has for the accounting department

(Note: The DPRs come in a little later than I like, so be prepared for that.)

Call sheets are published by the AD, and different ADs may set them up different ways. Regardless, on the front of the call sheet – which you'll get very familiar with – there should be a special extras section. This will give you a heads up on how many extras, officially called background actors except on commercials, are working that day.

In Chapter 17, where we'll look at all the production forms, I have included an example of what we call a skin (see page 192). Skins are top sheets with the names of the extras for the day, info on whether each extra was a stand-in, "special ability," or general background, and rates. These should be kept in the files.

When you get the extra vouchers, you'll need to match each one to its release form, a document from Business Affairs in which the extra gives permission to the production company to use their likeness in the film. Do read the release form so you know whether it covers only one day or the run of the show and whether you need to get a new release each time a given extra works.

If you're missing either a voucher or a release form, you need to let the payroll coordinator and the production coordinator know so it can be taken care of right away. Never pay the extra without the release form.

Once you match the voucher and release form, double-check them against the DPR and skins for the final extra count. That way, you can let the payroll coordinator know if the vouchers don't match the head count on the DPR. This also will let the accountant know if the count is over or under for the day — she'll need this as part of her hot cost number.

On the extra paperwork and release forms, make sure you have everyone's info. Extras' handwriting can be horrible, and they mess up their zip codes a lot of the time. If you are missing anything, you'll need to call them. Use the office land line. Never use your personal line, *or you'll be miserable and may require therapy.*

Make a note on the voucher with the time and date you left a message. Stay on top of this. If in two days you haven't heard back from them, email them. Then let the production coordinator know you've tried to get them the info, and make another list of all the missing details and share it with the payroll coordinator. Constantly update!

Bigger shows usually budget for an extras coordinator, and chances are if you see this in the budget, you will have a lot of extras to pay. The extras coordinator is responsible for double-checking all the paperwork. Sometimes things get missed and you will have to go straight to them to fix the problem.

Union and Non-Union Extras

(Please always check for updates on the SAG-AFTRA website, sagaftra.org.)

The next few pages give you an insight into how to calculate the vouchers, along with other things you'll need to know.

This information is reprinted from the 2020 *SAG-AFTRA Background Actors Contracts Digest* with permission (available for download at sagaftra.org/ backgroundactors). Some elements have been summarized, and the digest contains far more detail than I have included here. And remember, when you're looking up rates, you'll need to differentiate between extras (on commercials only) and background actors (on everything else). Even though our paperwork always says it's for extras, most of the shows you'll be on will actually have background actors instead. If you look up extras rates when what you need are background rates, you'll be using the wrong numbers for your calculations.

SAG-AFTRA has different contracts for radio, TV, game shows, and so forth. Look for the one you need.

Scope

Minimum number of covered background actors [*there are some exclusions, so please read up; these numbers are from 2019*]:

Features   57
Television   21

STAND-INS:

• One stand-in is included in the count of covered background actors in theatrical motion pictures.

• Stand-ins are included in the count of covered background actors in long-form television motion pictures.

• Three stand-ins per day shall be excluded from the count of covered background actors in short-form television ($^1/_2$-hour and 1-hour projects).

Definitions

GENERAL BACKGROUND: Person of atmospheric business which includes the normal actions, gestures, and facial expressions of the background actor's assignment.

SPECIAL ABILITY BACKGROUND ACTOR: Background actor specifically called and assigned to perform work requiring special skills such as tennis, golf, dancing (including square dancing), swimming, skating, riding animals, driving livestock, non-professional singing (in groups of 16 or less), mouthing to playback in groups of 16 or less, professional or organized athletic sports (including officiating and running), amputees, driving which requires a special skill and a special license (such as truck driving but not cab driving), motorcycle driving, insert work, and practical card dealing.

STAND-IN: Background actor used as a substitute for another actor for purposes of focusing shots, setting lights, etc., but not actually photographed. Stand-ins may also be used as general background.

PHOTO DOUBLE: Background actor who is photographed to substitute for another actor. A general background actor who is required to do photographic doubling shall receive the stand-in rate.

OMNIES: Any speech sounds used as general background noise rather than for its meaning. Atmospheric words such as indistinguishable background chatter in a party or restaurant scene [*e.g., "rhubarb, rhubarb, rhubarb"*].

Rates

MINIMUM DAILY RATE SCALE [*for an eight-hour day*]
AS OF 07/01/2019 THROUGH 06/30/2020

General Background Actor	$174.00
Special Ability	$184.00
Stand-In/Photo Double	$204.00

[*The rates go up every year July 1.*]

Payments in Addition to Basic Daily Rate

[*Make sure you have the EP Paymaster book. If you don't, call SAG-AFTRA for the latest version of this information and read up.*]

Hazardous Work
Wet Work/Smoke Work
Body Makeup, Skullcap, Hair Goods, Haircuts
Rehearsals
Costume Fittings
Wardrobe Allowance

Damage to Wardrobe or Property: A background actor must file a lost or damaged property report with producer prior to leaving the set. Producer must provide a form for the purpose of filing such claim.

Interview Fees

Background actors reporting for interviews shall receive an allowance for the first 2 hours of the interview in the amount of $^1/_4$ check. For time in excess of two hours, Background Actors shall be paid in units of 2 hours at the specified regular hourly rate for the call being filled.

In addition, background actors required to bring the following to an interview shall receive the indicated additional payment:

Requested wardrobe $^1/_2$ the applicable allowance rate
Requested pet, auto, prop $^1/_2$ the applicable allowance rate

Personal Props

Background actors required to furnish the following shall receive the indicated additional payments:

1) Pets, Personal Accessories — Allowances Per Day:
   [*Please see your copy of Digest for current rates.*]

2) For props not listed above, the Background Actor may negotiate a fee at time of booking.

3) Autos, Etc. — Allowances Per Day:
   [*Please see your copy of Digest for current rates.*]

Mileage is also due for all miles traveled by the background actor upon the producer's instructions.

[*In Los Angeles, mileage is computed from the producer's studio to any location within the studio zone. If not reporting to a studio, mileage is computed from the intersection of Beverly Boulevard and La Cienega to the location.*]

Sixteen-Hour Rule Violation [*AKA Force Call*]

The penalty for violation of the 16-hour rule (aka "golden time") is one day of pay for each hour (or fraction thereof). Meal breaks, wardrobe and prop return, and travel time are included in calculating 16 hours.

Meal Periods

Meal period must be at least half hour but not longer than one hour (and are not counted as part of paid work time). The first meal period shall be called not later than six hours from the time of call. All subsequent meal periods shall be called not later than 6 hours after the end of the preceding meal period.

ND meals (non-deductible meals) also known as NDB (non-deductible breakfast) may only be called within the first two hours of the background actor's call time. They are 15 minutes in length, during which the background actor must be free of all activity, including wardrobe, makeup and hair. Such ND meal must be a meal appropriate to the time of day, and must be given only for the purpose of aligning the background actor's meal times with the crew meal times.

THE PENALTIES FOR ANY VIOLATION OF THE
FOREGOING SHALL BE:

First $1/2$ hour of delay or fraction thereof	$ 7.50
Second $1/2$ hour of delay or fraction thereof	$10.00
Each additional $1/2$ hour of delay or fraction thereof	$12.50

[*There's a different rate for cast.*]

Overtime

The regular workday is 8 consecutive hours (excluding meal periods). The 9th and 10th hours are payable at time and one half in one-tenth hour (6-minute) units. Work beyond the 10th hour is payable at double-time in tenths of an hour (6-minute) units. [*This is California law.*]

Sixth and Seventh Day, and Holiday Worked

The regular studio workweek shall consist of any five (5) consecutive days out of any seven (7) consecutive days, commencing with the first of such five (5) days. However, the five (5) consecutive day requirement shall be deemed satisfied where on commencing employment, the Background Actor is assigned to a schedule that calls for him/her to work, for example, on Monday and Tuesday, with Wednesday and Thursday as the regular days off, and is followed by work on Friday through the following Tuesday.

All work performed on a 6th consecutive day for the same employer shall be paid at the rate of 1½ times the background actor's daily rate (except on an overnight location 6th consecutive day is paid at straight time).

All work performed on a 7th consecutive day for the same employer shall be paid at the rate of double the background actor's daily rate (except on an overnight location 7th consecutive day is paid at 1½ times).

Holidays

New Year's Day, Presidents Day, Good Friday, Memorial Day, Independence Day, Labor Day, Thanksgiving Day, the day after Thanksgiving Day, and Christmas Day shall be recognized as holidays. If any of the above holidays falls on a Saturday, the preceding Friday shall be considered the holiday, and if a holiday falls on Sunday, the following Monday shall be considered the holiday, except that on overnight locations, Saturday holidays will be recognized on Saturday.

Provisions for Holidays Not Worked

Studio employment: Allowance of one day's pay at straight time if the background actor is employed by producer the day before and after any of the above named nine holidays.

Provisions for Holidays Worked

Double daily wage. Overtime premium payments shall not be compounded or pyramided and shall be paid at the highest applicable premium rate only.

The contract digest changes most years, so please download the current version rather than relying on this information.

SOME SITUATIONS THAT AFFECT PAY:
• Nudity
• Working in a higher classification
• Cancellations
• Weather-permitting calls

There is way more to read on MINORS. But as a clerk, you will not deal with this. Minors are the responsibility of the production coordinator and the payroll coordinator.

You can find blank examples of union and non-union extra vouchers in Chapter 17. In addition to a voucher, you'll need a W-4 and an I-9 from each extra.

Always make sure all fields are filled out.

W-4

This is only to be filled out the first time someone works on the production or if their info changes in the time frame they are working. If they work more than one day, after the first day they only fill out the voucher time card section.

Along with this form is the extras release form. As I mentioned, read this to see if the form covers only the day they worked or all days down the line. This way you'll know whether you need one with each extra voucher, every single day, or whether you only need them from extras who are on their first day on set.

Chapter 10

Clerk Work: Helping the First Assistant

Now that you're a payroll expert, let's talk about the things you'll be helping the first assistant accountant with if time allows.

Managing Department Inboxes

Remember those inboxes you set up by the door when you first moved in to your office? Time to tackle those.

Sort all the inbox items into A/P, POs, PC, P-cards, start paperwork, time cards, and so on. Alphabetize and stack each type of item. This should leave you with six stacks:
1) A/P invoices that have been emailed or mailed in
2) New POs with backups and W-9s attached
3) PC envelopes that have been turned in
4) P-cards that have been turned in
5) New start forms for crew, cast, or extras
6) Time cards

You might not have all of these items every day, of course. Your stacks will vary depending on what has arrived since the last time you sorted the boxes.

Go through the mail, paperclipping any invoices you find to the mailing envelopes provided with them. You will also have received some invoices via email — on the POs we create, I include a line that says in huge font: **EMAIL ALL INVOICES AND W-9S TO Showname_AP@GMAIL.COM** — so check that email daily for all incoming A/P and print out the invoices attached.

In Chapter 5, I briefly mentioned the different stamps you will need. Among them is the approval stamp. I create mine on Excel and take them to Staples to have them made.

Stamp the invoices for approval (be careful not to stamp over the stub or block any text). Don't forget to fill in the approval stamp!

Approval Stamps for All Invoices

(Actual size is smaller to fit on the invoices)

PO#: It should be clear by now what this one means!

CODING (AKA account code or GL code): The account this invoice is going to be coded to. Get the budget code from the budget or the cost report in the accounting software. (If you can't find it on the CR, try the budget — it's more detailed. I usually keep both on hand.)

APPROVAL STAMP	
PO #	
CODING	
(OV)/UNDER ETC	
LP APPVL	
ACCT. APPVL	
AMT LEFT ON PO	

OVER/UNDER ETC: On the cost report, go to the estimate to complete column and find the GL code, deduct the invoice amount from the ETC, and see if the amount available is negative or positive.

What does a negative amount look like? Let's say the ETC column reads -$400.55, the invoice is for $125.00, and there is no new PO. Subtract the invoice amount from the ETC, and the new ETC will be -$525.55. You are now $525.55 over budget in that area.

If the ETC is (positive) $400.55, then your new ETC would be $275.55; there was money in the account, you've deducted the new amount from it, and the production has $275.55 left available for this code.

You only enter the invoice in the software if a PO is **not entered in the system**. There's no need to change the ETC, because it automatically adjusts in the software when you enter the invoice, but you do need to change the stamp.

If there is a PO in the system and the amount matches the invoice, then the ETC stays where it is, whether its amount is negative or positive. Fill in the PO amount on the spot on the approval stamp marked "Amt left on PO." Make sure you organize all your POs by code while you are entering them, so that you are keeping accurate track of how much money you have left in the account you are coding the PO in.

LP APPVL: Line producer's approval

ACCT. APPVL: Accountant's approval

AMT LEFT ON PO: The amount of the PO remaining to be paid after you deduct the invoice in your hand. The software automatically does this when you enter the invoice.

Meet Your New Best Friend: The Indexed Sorter

Indexed Sorter, Index Tab Style: A–Z; numbers 0–30,000 and 1–31;
Monday to Sunday; January to December
Number of Leaves/Dividers: 31

This will help you alphabetize the documents.

You should not be Cinderella (*pre-ball*) when helping the payroll coordinator or first assistant. I don't allow this in my department. I always keep my eyes and ears open so that they don't take advantage of you. You are only getting a taste of each accounting job to help you decide in which direction you want to go. No one wants to be a clerk FOREVER.

Purchase Orders

The purpose of a PO is to enter a place saver in the estimate to complete column on the cost report and to know if you have either a saving or an overage in that budget account. You'll also need to check them against the A/P invoices that come in via mail or email.

Purchase orders are generated by department heads or department coordinators. They are signed out by the clerk to those departments and the numbers are tracked in Excel.

EXAMPLES OF DEPARTMENTS THAT GET PO'S:
- Wardrobe
- Props
- Art Department (coordinator for the set-dressing department)
- Hair
- Makeup
- Transportation (which has a transportation coordinator)
- Craft Service
- Construction (which has its own construction coordinator, hopefully)

ALL OF THE ABOVE DO THEIR OWN PO'S, WHICH THEY SHOULD BE TURNING IN TO YOU AS THEY ORDER ITEMS, WITH BACKUP AND A W-9.

Here is a sample of a PO log, which the clerk is responsible for.

EXAMPLE

EXAMPLE			Purchase order log		
Acctg Productions					
Date	PO #	Dept	Signed out to	Descriptions	Amount
2/20/2019	1120	Sound	Jason Coord.	Batteries	$625.00
2/20/2019	1121	Prods.	Jason Coord.	TBD	
2/20/2019	1122	Prods.	Jason Coord.	TBD	
2/20/2019	1123	Prods.	Jason Coord.	TBD	
2/20/2019	1124	Prods.	Jason Coord.	TBD	
2/21/2019	1125	Prods.	Jason Coord.	Void	$0.00
2/21/2019	1126	Prods.	Return		$0.00
		ETC.			
				Grand Total:	$625.00

The production coordinator is responsible for production POs, such as anything needed for the best boy grip, best boy electric, camera, sound, and other items. Sometimes, if we're lucky enough, the best boy grip and best boy electric will write their own POs out.

Purchase orders are to be turned in as the items are ordered, and turned in daily. Please make sure the people you are giving blank POs to understand this and also know that they are not to throw away the voided or blank ones. If they void a PO, those need to be turned in, in one piece, and at the end of the show any blank ones need to be returned to you. And double-check that they know how to fill out a PO.

When you've received the day's POs and you take them out of the inbox, organize them into alphabetical order along with their corresponding W-9s or W-8-BENs (the international equivalent of the US W-9) and backup quotes.

If a PO doesn't have an attached W-9 (first check your W-9 file or binder to see if it's in there), email or call the vendor and have them send the missing form ASAP so you can enter it.

A W-9 is very important when you're setting up the vendor because this will determine if they get a 1099 at the end of the year. And you don't want to screw up on taxes! We'll go into 1099s in the next chapter, so don't worry if you don't know what I'm talking about yet.

Separate your alphabetized POs into completed documents and incompletes (missing backup, W-9, or W-8-BEN). Go through each PO and double-check the math on it. Then double-check the backup to make sure that the amounts were picked up correctly and multiplied out correctly.

Once you know the PO and W-9 match the backup and all the math is good, then you can code your PO. (I personally give the clerk a copy of the budget for expenses only so they can see the budget codes.)

Then it's time to enter the W-9. Miss C. Kampfur has a pretty good video demonstrating how to do this; she's using software called QuickBooks, which is not what you'll be using, but this is a good overview of the basic principles:

https://www.youtube.com/watch?v=7JrYg2cfTIo

And here's another example from Entertainment Partners' YouTube channel, using Global Vista production accounting software:

https://www.youtube.com/watch?v=_exnTIk2Q8g

Some more videos:

https://www.youtube.com/user/BroadcastEP/videos

Use the PO and the backup to figure out what the default tax code will be when you enter the vendor for the first time (see page 90). This will depend on what we're paying for: rental, labor, lawyer, etc.

Now that you've separated out your complete and incomplete POs and coded the complete ones, you can paperclip each PO separately, assembled this way:

THE GOOD STACK: PO, backup, approval from department that wrote the PO, and W-9.

THE BAD STACK: PO, Post-it note explaining what you're missing. Then start calling and get what you need from the vendor.

Place the good stack in the "AP/PO for approval" folder. Now, if you see an invoice for the full amount of the PO, that PO should be voided and labeled with a note, "PO came in at the same time as invoice." Do not throw away the voided PO. Enter it on your PO log as voided and then put it in the "to be filed" inbox.

If you have an invoice for a partial payment and the new PO is for the full amount (check this against the quote), you may need to adjust the PO. Or just enter the full PO into the software first, then enter the invoice, select your PO, and the program will automatically deduct that amount from the PO total, called drawing down.

EXAMPLE:
You have a PO for ABC prop rentals; the amount is $6,000.00 ($750.00 x eight weeks). You also have an invoice for $750.00, which is rental for one of the weeks referenced on the PO.

Deduct the $750.00 from the full amount of the PO.

The PO that you now need to enter is $5,250.00. Write out the invoice on the back of the PO in the draw-down section, with the correct rental dates adjusted (see page 185).

Now it's time to distribute the copies of the PO, once it's been approved by the accountant and LP and entered in the log and the software.

The original copy (white) goes to the vendor or the person who filled the PO out, along with a backup copy.

The yellow copy goes in an accordion folder where you house all of your completed, approved, and entered POs, in alphabetical order with a backup, awaiting invoice to match.

The goldenrod copy goes to the production coordinator with a backup.

The pink copy goes in the file cabinet in numerical order (no backup needed).

If your POs are digital, use the same distributions as above. Nothing gets distributed until it is approved and entered.

When you enter the PO in the accounting software, it gives you two description spots. The first description line is for the rental dates or service dates. The second description line should be the item. If it's a big list of items, pick the big-ticket items and enter those using abbreviations. Please, try not to use the same description on multiple POs in the software — that will make it very hard to keep track of which was which.

If the PO is for a purchase, you'll need to find out the asset amount the production company or studio has in place. An **asset** is something the company or studio owns, worth more than a certain value. Each company or studio might have a different asset limit.

For example, say your production has an asset limit of $300.00. Anything you buy for the production worth more than that amount needs to be tracked. So, let's say the production goes to Best Buy to purchase a TV and other items. Along with the TV itself, the receipt shows the purchase of miscellaneous office supplies, and the total is $665.75. You would mark an A on the receipt (for *asset*), and your entry in the software would be this:

"Best Buy_Sanyo 35 TV_$425.65"
The TV cost more than $300.00, so you mark the free field, which is labeled "FF" in the software, with the A for asset.

The rest of your $665.75 receipt entry would be:
"Best Buy_Misc. Office Supplies_$240.10 for the balance"

You don't enter an A for that, since it's less than the asset limit.

At the end of the show, you'll print out the asset list. All the items on it must be returned to production, the studio, or whatever their guidelines call for. The rest of the purchased items get boxed up and labeled in case of a reshoot.

When you're done entering the POs, stamp all the pages with the "entered" stamp in the same place, so when you record the transaction number, it's in the right place on each PO copy.

Feel ready to handle POs? I hope so, because we're moving on to...

Chapter 11

1099s: Who, What, When, Where, Why?

Let's talk taxes! Everyone's least favorite subject – except for accountants (that's you)! Love them or hate them, you're going to be working on them, so best get familiar with the forms that are relevant on all productions.

We'll start with 1099s. If you've never been an independent contractor, you may never have encountered the 1099 before, but they're part of every production and you need to understand them.

Before you begin work on a year's 1099s, you have to make sure that a cutoff check-printing date is set. I usually let all vendors and independent contractors know that no check will be cut from December 15th through the end of the first week in January. This ensures that all the checks have been cut before the end of the year, which makes taxes much easier on everyone and leaves a very simple end-of-year cleanup for the corporate finance officer (CFO).

WHAT IS A 1099 AND WHEN IS ONE REQUIRED?

Let's start with an example:

Charlie spends four weeks over the summer working as a driver for a movie. Little paperwork was required when Charlie received the job. Management told Charlie he would make $20/hour and work approximately twenty-five hours a week. And it gets even better – no taxes are taken out of Charlie's check. "Awesome!!" Charlie thinks when he cashes his first check. "I get to keep all this money for myself!!" *Oh, silly Charlie.*

But January rolls around and Charlie receives a letter in the mail. "**Important Tax Document Enclosed**" is written on the medium-sized envelope. Charlie opens it and pulls out two pieces of paper, roughly 8.5 x 5.5 inches. He notices the document lists all his information: his full name, address, Social Security number. Charlie sees the information of the company he worked for as well: address, phone number, and tax ID number, called the TIN.

An amount appears on the document: $2,000, the amount Charlie made working as a driver last year. Both pieces of paper look the same. They

PAYER'S name, street address, city or town, state or province, country, ZIP or foreign postal code, and telephone no.	1 Rents $	OMB No. 1545-0115	
GENERIC MOVIE TITLE, LLC 7878 DRIVING CENTER LN CHARLIELAND, CA 98393	2 Royalties $	20**16** Form **1099-MISC**	**Miscellaneous Income**
	3 Other income $	4 Federal income tax withheld $	**Copy B For Recipient**
PAYER'S federal identification number 12-1212121	RECIPIENT'S identification number 123-45-6789	5 Fishing boat proceeds $	6 Medical and health care payments $	
RECIPIENT'S name CHARLIE DRIVEMAN		7 Nonemployee compensation $2,000.00	8 Substitute payments in lieu of dividends or interest $	This is important tax information and is being furnished to the Internal Revenue Service. If you are required to file a return, a negligence penalty or other sanction may be imposed on you if this income is taxable and the IRS determines that it has not been reported.
Street address (including apt. no.) 12345 MAIN ST		9 Payer made direct sales of $5,000 or more of consumer products to a buyer (recipient) for resale ▶ $	10 Crop insurance proceeds $	
City or town, state or province, country, and ZIP or foreign postal code CHARLIELAND, CA 98393		11	12	
Account number (see instructions)	FATCA filing requirement	13 Excess golden parachute payments $	14 Gross proceeds paid to an attorney $	
15a Section 409A deferrals $	15b Section 409A income $	16 State tax withheld $ $	17 State/Payer's state no.	18 State income $ $

Form **1099-MISC**   (keep for your records)   www.irs.gov/form1099misc   Department of the Treasury - Internal Revenue Service

Image I: Sample 1099

both show Charlie's full name and address and the company's information. But on the far right-hand side, the documents differ. One document reads "Copy B: For recipient," and the other reads "Copy 2: To be filed with recipient's state income tax return when required."

Everyone, let's all give Charlie a round of applause, because he just received a 1099! And he's going to have to pay taxes on it! *Welcome to the real world, Charlie.*

So, what is a **1099**? (*Hint: That giant image on the previous page.*)

Charlie thinks back to his prior working experience, where he received other tax documents in the mail in January reviewing his earnings from the previous year. But this document looks different. It just says how much money Charlie made. There's no information about how much money was withheld for federal and state taxes. Charlie is thinking of a **W-2**, which is only for employees of the company or anyone run through the payroll for the production company.

Several of you reading this might be thinking, "Charlie worked for the company. He's an employee." Well, no. As a matter of fact, the section where Charlie's earnings for the year are displayed is labeled "non-employee compensation." Calling Charlie an employee would be incorrect. A more accurate description of him would be a freelancer or an independent contractor.

WHO ACTUALLY GETS A 1099?

Short answer: Everything and everyone that is not a corporation and was paid over $600 by a company or business.

What about LLCs that are S/C corporations? The rule of thumb is that anything that is a corporation does not get 1099'ed. However, there is no

Form **W-9** (Rev. November 2017) Department of the Treasury Internal Revenue Service	**Request for Taxpayer** **Identification Number and Certification** ▶ Go to *www.irs.gov/FormW9* for instructions and the latest information.	Give Form to the requester. Do not send to the IRS.

1 Name (as shown on your income tax return). Name is required on this line; do not leave this line blank.

CHARLIE DRIVEMAN

2 Business name/disregarded entity name, if different from above

N/A

3 Check appropriate box for federal tax classification of the person whose name is entered on line 1. Check only **one** of the following seven boxes.

- ☑ Individual/sole proprietor or single-member LLC
- ☐ C Corporation
- ☐ S Corporation
- ☐ Partnership
- ☐ Trust/estate

☐ Limited liability company. Enter the tax classification (C=C corporation, S=S corporation, P=Partnership) ▶ _____

Note: Check the appropriate box in the line above for the tax classification of the single-member owner. Do not check LLC if the LLC is classified as a single-member LLC that is disregarded from the owner unless the owner of the LLC is another LLC that is **not** disregarded from the owner for U.S. federal tax purposes. Otherwise, a single-member LLC that is disregarded from the owner should check the appropriate box for the tax classification of its owner.

☐ Other (see instructions) ▶ _____

4 Exemptions (codes apply only to certain entities, not individuals; see instructions on page 3):

Exempt payee code (if any) _____

Exemption from FATCA reporting code (if any) _____

(Applies to accounts maintained outside the U.S.)

5 Address (number, street, and apt. or suite no.) See instructions.

12345 MAIN ST.

6 City, state, and ZIP code

CHARLIELAND, CA, 98393

Requester's name and address (optional)

7 List account number(s) here (optional)

Print or type.
See Specific Instructions on page 3.

Part I   **Taxpayer Identification Number (TIN)**

Enter your TIN in the appropriate box. The TIN provided must match the name given on line 1 to avoid backup withholding. For individuals, this is generally your social security number (SSN). However, for a resident alien, sole proprietor, or disregarded entity, see the instructions for Part I, later. For other entities, it is your employer identification number (EIN). If you do not have a number, see *How to get a TIN*, later.

Note: If the account is in more than one name, see the instructions for line 1. Also see *What Name and Number To Give the Requester* for guidelines on whose number to enter.

Social security number

1 2 3 – 4 5 – 6 7 8 9

or

Employer identification number

_ _ – _ _ _ _ _ _ _

Part II   **Certification**

Under penalties of perjury, I certify that:

1. The number shown on this form is my correct taxpayer identification number (or I am waiting for a number to be issued to me); and
2. I am not subject to backup withholding because: (a) I am exempt from backup withholding, or (b) I have not been notified by the Internal Revenue Service (IRS) that I am subject to backup withholding as a result of a failure to report all interest or dividends, or (c) the IRS has notified me that I am no longer subject to backup withholding; and
3. I am a U.S. citizen or other U.S. person (defined below); and
4. The FATCA code(s) entered on this form (if any) indicating that I am exempt from FATCA reporting is correct.

Certification instructions. You must cross out item 2 above if you have been notified by the IRS that you are currently subject to backup withholding because you have failed to report all interest and dividends on your tax return. For real estate transactions, item 2 does not apply. For mortgage interest paid, acquisition or abandonment of secured property, cancellation of debt, contributions to an individual retirement arrangement (IRA), and generally, payments other than interest and dividends, you are not required to sign the certification, but you must provide your correct TIN. See the instructions for Part II, later.

Sign Here   Signature of U.S. person ▶   CHARLIE DRIVEMAN   Date ▶   FEBRUARY 32, 2019

General Instructions

Section references are to the Internal Revenue Code unless otherwise noted.

Future developments. For the latest information about developments related to Form W-9 and its instructions, such as legislation enacted after they were published, go to *www.irs.gov/FormW9*.

Purpose of Form

An individual or entity (Form W-9 requester) who is required to file an information return with the IRS must obtain your correct taxpayer identification number (TIN) which may be your social security number (SSN), individual taxpayer identification number (ITIN), adoption taxpayer identification number (ATIN), or employer identification number (EIN), to report on an information return the amount paid to you, or other amount reportable on an information return. Examples of information returns include, but are not limited to, the following.

- Form 1099-INT (interest earned or paid)
- Form 1099-DIV (dividends, including those from stocks or mutual funds)
- Form 1099-MISC (various types of income, prizes, awards, or gross proceeds)
- Form 1099-B (stock or mutual fund sales and certain other transactions by brokers)
- Form 1099-S (proceeds from real estate transactions)
- Form 1099-K (merchant card and third party network transactions)
- Form 1098 (home mortgage interest), 1098-E (student loan interest), 1098-T (tuition)
- Form 1099-C (canceled debt)
- Form 1099-A (acquisition or abandonment of secured property)

Use Form W-9 only if you are a U.S. person (including a resident alien), to provide your correct TIN.

If you do not return Form W-9 to the requester with a TIN, you might be subject to backup withholding. See What is backup withholding, later.

Cat. No. 10231X   Form **W-9** (Rev. 11-2017)

Image 2: Charlie's W-9

penalty for 1099'ing a corporation. There IS a penalty for not issuing a 1099 to someone who should receive one.

So, to summarize: 1099s are issued to people who make more than $600 of non-taxed income working for a company or business throughout the course of the year. Companies that are not corporations receive 1099s as well. 1099s differ from W-2s because no taxes are withheld.

I certainly hope Charlie didn't spend that entire $2,000.

But how did we get here? How did our driving friend go from working for this film company to receiving a 1099 months later? In the previous chapter, there were two videos that showed the process of entering a W-9. I cannot stress enough how important it is to enter a W-9 correctly. Misidentifying a corporation could be the difference between sending and not sending a 1099 to someone who should receive one. This will cause major headaches down the road.

Bernadette L. Harris's YouTube channel has an informative video explaining 1099s:

https://www.youtube.com/watch?v=O3c2yzew0f4

By the way, printing 1099s is only your responsibility on small shows. On studio shows, either the studio has the payroll company do the final 1099s (for a fee) or someone at corporate gets to do them. Setting up the W-9s is always your responsibility, though. Fun times.

See that vendor entry image on the next page? A couple of things to note:
1. In the box labeled "Tax," an option exists for corporations, but not individuals, LLCs, partnerships, etc. For individuals or companies that require a 1099, check the 1099 box. (Hooray for simplicity!)
2. 1099/T4A: Though slightly abbreviated in the image, it reads "Non-

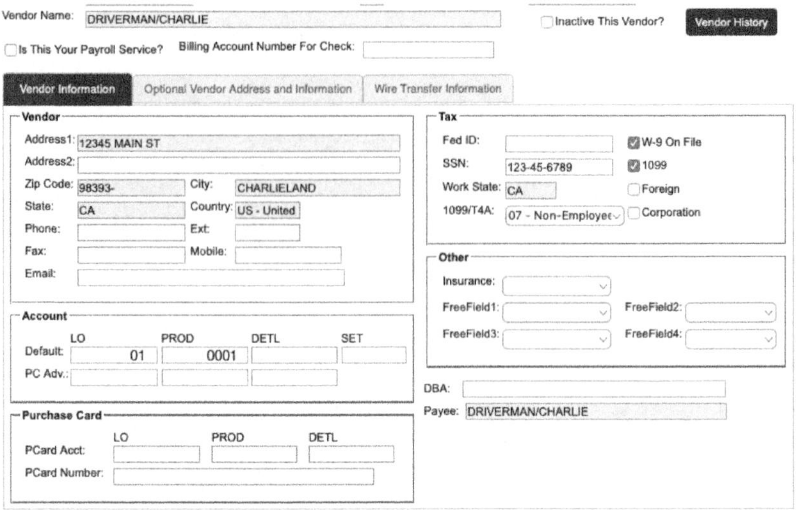

Image 3: Screenshot of the vendor entry page from MediaWeb Software *Reprint courtesy of Media Services Payroll*

employee compensation." Every one of Charlie's checks will have that written on it, therefore his 1099 at the end of the year will have all his earnings listed in Box 7. We will get to this later.

3. Remember budget codes? Presumably, drivers were budgeted, and there should be a code for them. This would be written under "DETL" in the account box.

4. To set a default production and location code, set them up in your vendor entry window; those will never change on your show. In the example above, we've set the location code to 01 and the production code to 0001.

5. Also note the option to say if you have the vendor's W-9 on file. If you have it on file – AND YOU SHOULD – click the box. (Duh?)

6. Charlieland was the best I could think of. *Funkytown was already taken.*

It's the End of the Year

So, January rolls around and it's time to issue Charlie's 1099. The first step, and prepare to have your mind blown, is... buy the 1099 supplies! Any Staples or Office Depot will have what you need. Pick up the "1099-Misc." forms. The packets you're looking for should have five separate sets of forms attached:

Form A

Form B

Form 2

Form C (two sets of this one)

Form 1096

We'll go over what each form is soon.

Also, make sure you pick up enough envelopes – the 1099-Misc. "peel and seal" envelopes. A twenty-five pack will do.

So, you have purchased the supplies. What next? Generate the 1099 report! What is the 1099 report? Essentially, it is a rundown of every single A/P check that was written throughout the year. Your software will give you all sorts of options to click when generating a report. You can include corporations, people making under $600, which fiscal year you want a report for, and how much information you want to see from each vendor. Include only taxable income or income that is both taxable and non-taxable.

DETAILED VS. SUMMARY REPORT:

What is the difference between a detailed report and a summary report? A detailed report is, well, more detailed. Both forms have all the necessary W-9 information: TIN, W-9 on file, is the vendor 1099'ed or not, are they a corporation or not. But the difference is that on a detailed report, you get every single transaction for the vendor, meaning everything that they were paid.

When correcting coding mistakes, a detailed report allows us to find errors more easily, and it also gives us an immense amount of information to help us find the transactions that need changing. For end-of-year 1099s, detailed reports are what you want to use. You also get the vendor's address on a detailed report, which is definitely something you will want to check.

We only care about Charlie today, so after selecting the type of report and how much we want to see, we can unselect all other vendors and look at just Charlie. It makes him feel special.

MAKE SURE THE TIN IS FILLED IN:
On the 1099 report, there should be a place where it says "TIN." To remind you, this stands for "tax identification number." *Make sure this is filled in for all vendors!* You will not be able to generate a 1099 without this information. If the vendor doesn't have an official TIN, fill in their Social Security number instead. Make sure the address is filled in as well.

Yes, before cutting an A/P check, a W-9 should have been filled out, but sometimes checks need to be issued ASAP and steps can be missed in the rush. If you see incomplete information for vendors on these 1099 reports, make a note of it and contact those people for a W-9. Honestly, before you change a single 1099 code, this should be the first thing you do.

After years of 1099 experience, I start the job in the middle of December. Whether you're staff or freelance, if you're around in December, start this process two weeks before you leave for the year, double-checking that the vendors were set up correctly and 1099 codes were entered correctly. Never assume this, especially if you were hired to replace someone. Reach out to people and companies for their W-9s now, because in late December and early January, Los Angeles shuts down. Getting someone to send you a 1099 is going to be next to impossible. **DO NOT** slack on this.

So, all of Charlie's information looks good. What else do we check? The 1099 code. We'll only deal with three of the codes for now. Really, only two of them are your primary concern (01 and 07). Code 03 will come up occasionally.

01: This code is used for rentals. This comes up frequently, and it's likely to be the one you deal with most often. Renting equipment? Code as 01. Renting property where your cast and crew stay during the shoot? Code as 01. You get the idea.

07: This code is used for labor. Charlie's work as a driver for four weeks would be classified as 07. So, Charlie's 1099 would have the entire $2,000 he made that month in Box 7.

Can you have multiple boxes filled out on a 1099? Absolutely! If the company needed some carpet cleaning done once a month and Charlie agreed to rent the company his carpet cleaner for $100 a time, in addition to the $2,000 in Box 7, Charlie's 1099 would have $1,200 in Box 1.

The 03 code will not come up much, but there are a couple instances where you will need to use it. The 03 code is used for... well, it's a little tricky. Check with the CPA of the company you are working with, if in doubt.

Let's say I'm working for a movie that houses its cast and crew. All these properties require a deposit. One of the house owners is named Lucy. I rent her house for $3,000 a month and our rental agreement stipulates a $3,000 deposit up front. Lucy is not a corporation, so she gets 1099'ed at the end of the year for $39,000, all of it in Box 01 for rentals. NOPE!!! $36,000 goes in Box 01 (for the twelve months of rent at $3,000/month) and $3,000 in 03, for the deposit. "But the $3,000 is a rental." Really? That money is not for rent, and it's obviously not labor. So, we place that amount in 03.

Code 03 does not come up often, but every now and then you will have to deal with it.

The Reimbursement Question

EXAMPLE: Charlie not only gets paid his $2,000 total income, but one week he also picks up lunch for the company and gets reimbursed. So, at the end of the year Charlie has been paid $2,239.75, but only $2,000 appears on his 1099. What gives? Reimbursements are not 1099'ed, because they are not income and therefore not taxable. Make sure when writing a check you are as specific as possible. If Charlie's invoice is for $739.75 the week he picks up lunch, make sure the check reflects all the charges.

Remember the importance of selecting "Detailed Report"?

1099	V1099	Amount	Description	
07 - N		500.00	5 days driving - $100	
		239.75	lunch reimb	

Image 4: Charlie's A/P check entry
(*make sure his labor and reimbursements are on separate lines — DO NOT GET LAZY WHEN DOING THIS!!!*)

This is why you read a detailed 1099 report and make sure you click the "taxable and non-taxable" option. Untaxed reimbursements and things like them would not show up on a 1099 summary report. Seeing all the money vendors were paid throughout the year ensures that no one is 1099'ed for money they should not be. And it also allows you to see every transaction, perhaps finding money that has not been 1099'ed but should be.

What's With All These Forms?

Charlie's TIN is correct, his address is correct, the amount Charlie made during the year is correct and in the right 1099 box. Now what the heck do I print?

Remember I mentioned five forms earlier? No? I did. I totally did.

What is each form?
Form A: Goes to the IRS
Form B: Goes to the employee
Form 2: Goes to the employee

Do Not Staple   6969

Form 1096

Department of the Treasury
Internal Revenue Service

Annual Summary and Transmittal of U.S. Information Returns

OMB No. 1545-0108

2019

FILER'S name

GENERIC MOVIE TITLE, LLC

Street address (including room or suite number)

7878 DRIVING CENTER LN

City or town, state or province, country, and ZIP or foreign postal code

CHARLIELAND, CA 98393

Name of person to contact	Telephone number	For Official Use Only
MR. ACCOUNTANT	123-456-7890	
Email address	Fax number	
MR.ACCOUNTANT.2019@GMAIL.COM	098-765-4321	

1 Employer identification number	2 Social security number	3 Total number of forms	4 Federal income tax withheld	5 Total amount reported with this Form 1096
12-1212121		1	$	$2,000.00

6 Enter an "X" in only one box below to indicate the type of form being filed.

7 Form 1099-MISC with NEC in box 7, check ▶ ☐

W-2G 32	1097-BTC 50	1098 81	1098-C 78	1098-E 84	1098-F 03	1098-Q 74	1098-T 83	1099-A 80	1099-B 79	1099-C 85	1099-CAP 73	1099-DIV 91	1099-G 86	1099-INT 92	1099-K 10	1099-LS 16
☐	☐	☐	☐	☐	☐	☐	☐	☐	☐	☐	☐	☐	☐	☐	☐	☐

1099-LTC 93	1099-MISC 95	1099-OID 96	1099-PATR 97	1099-Q 31	1099-QA 1A	1099-R 98	1099-S 75	1099-SA 94	1099-SB 43	3921 25	3922 26	5498 28	5498-ESA 72	5498-QA 2A	5498-SA 27
☐	☒	☐	☐	☐	☐	☐	☐	☐	☐	☐	☐	☐	☐	☐	☐

Return this entire page to the Internal Revenue Service. Photocopies are not acceptable.

Under penalties of perjury, I declare that I have examined this return and accompanying documents, and, to the best of my knowledge and belief, they are true, correct, and complete.

Signature ▶   MR. ACCOUNTANT   Title ▶   ACCOUNTANT   Date ▶   2/20/2019

Instructions

Future developments. For the latest information about developments related to Form 1096, such as legislation enacted after it was published, go to www.irs.gov/Form1096.

Reminder. The only acceptable method of electronically filing information returns listed on this form in box 6 with the IRS is through the FIRE System. See Pub. 1220.

Purpose of form. Use this form to transmit paper Forms 1097, 1098, 1099, 3921, 3922, 5498, and W-2G to the IRS.

Caution: If you are required to file 250 or more information returns of any one type, you must file electronically. If you are required to file electronically but fail to do so, and you do not have an approved waiver, you may be subject to a penalty. For more information, see part F in the 2019 General Instructions for Certain Information Returns.

Forms 1099-QA and 5498-QA can be filed on paper only, regardless of the number of returns.

Who must file. Any person or entity who files any of the forms shown in line 6 above must file Form 1096 to transmit those forms to the IRS.

Enter the filer's name, address (including room, suite, or other unit number), and taxpayer identification number (TIN) in the spaces provided on the form. The name, address, and TIN of the filer on this form must be the same as those you enter in the upper left area of Forms 1097, 1098, 1099, 3921, 3922, 5498, or W-2G.

When to file. File Form 1096 as follows.

• With Forms 1097, 1098, 1099, 3921, 3922, or W-2G, file by February 28, 2020.

Caution: We recommend you file Form 1099-MISC, as a **stand-alone** shipment, by January 31, 2020, if you are reporting **nonemployee compensation (NEC)** in box 7. Also, check box 7 above.

• With Forms 5498, file by June 1, 2020.

Where To File

Send all information returns filed on paper with Form 1096 to the following.

If your principal business, office or agency, or legal residence in the case of an individual, is located in	Use the following address
Alabama, Arizona, Arkansas, Delaware, Florida, Georgia, Kentucky, Maine, Massachusetts, Mississippi, New Hampshire, New Jersey, New Mexico, New York, North Carolina, Ohio, Texas, Vermont, Virginia	Department of the Treasury Internal Revenue Service Center Austin, TX 73301

For more information and the Privacy Act and Paperwork Reduction Act Notice, see the 2019 General Instructions for Certain Information Returns.

Cat. No. 14400O   Form **1096** (2019)

Image 5: Sample 1096

Form C: Stays with the company

Form 1096: This acts as a cover page for all the 1099s you send to the IRS (keep a copy per company for your files as well)

You will need the following information to fill out Form 1096:

Production company name

Production company address

Production company TIN

Accounting contact name and contact information

How many 1099s were sent

How much money was 1099'ed

The type of form being filed (Box 6 – in our case it will be 1099-Misc.)

Generating 1096s

Most accounting software will allow you to autogenerate 1096s (some don't, so you'll need to know how to write them by hand as well). In my experience, 1096s can be autogenerated incorrectly – the software can check the wrong box – so always double-check the 1096s and make sure when you fill out 1099s that the software checks the 1099 box on your 1096 form as well.

"Hey, Brody, if I hand write the 1096s, where do I get the information from?"

"That info comes from the software. You can print a 1096 on regular paper and transfer the information over to a blank form from the 1099 packet. Glad you asked."

Earlier I mentioned that you can choose how much information you would like to see on your 1099 reports. After you have finished filling in 1099s, the production company may ask you to print out a final 1099 report. This document will only show what has been 1099'ed. At the bottom of the last page, you will see a total amount for what was 1099'ed and how many vendors received the form.

A couple of things to note about the 1096:

1. The information on the 1099 Charlie received should match the information here if he's the only person you 1099'ed on the production. Otherwise, it should match the final 1099 report you printed out from the software.
2. Make sure the box for 1099-Misc. is checked.
3. Since, in our example, we are only concerned with Charlie's 1099, the total number of forms should read "1," and the amount should read $2,000.00 (the amount on Charlie's 1099).
4. I added a fake fax number because I guess people still have fax machines? Leaving this blank is fine, but make sure the accountant's information is on there.

We are now ready to print the 1099s. But when we do, we are given two options: print 1099s on pre-prepared forms or not. Since you bought all the 1099 forms, select the option to print on prepared 1099 forms.

Everything is now printed. What goes where? Take forms B and 2, place them in one of the envelopes, seal it, and Charlie will soon receive his 1099! He loves getting mail.

PLEASE NOTE:

• If you are printing hundreds of 1099s, print page 1 and make sure everything is correct. 1099 forms are printed in portrait, but 1099 reports are printed in landscape, so make sure you switch to the correct format and the margins are correct. See which option works best: printing to fit the page, printing in actual size, and so on. Make sure the 1099 paper is placed in the printer facing the right way. You have come this far and been incredibly detail-oriented. DO NOT GET LAZY when printing.

• Earlier, I mentioned that every individual 1099 has the contact information for the accounting department. Make sure every single 1099 has the most up-to-date information. If you work for a company that has made several movies over the past few years, chances are different accountants worked at different times. A 1099 with the phone number of an accountant who has not worked at the company in the last two years does absolutely no good for someone who has questions about his 1099. Make sure you talk to someone at the company (assuming it is not you) who can be the point person on all things 1099 during the next year and use that person's number on the forms.

• Make sure the address is visible in the window of the envelope.

• Mail out the 1099s to employees as soon as you can, but wait until the end of February before mailing anything to the IRS. Give employees ample time to check their 1099s and contact you if any information needs to be changed.

CORRECTING MISTAKES
For additional reading on how to deal with 1099 mistakes, consult the IRS handbook, which also lists the penalties for filing incorrect 1099s: https://www.irs.gov/pub/irs-pdf/i1099gi.pdf

1099-NEC

As of 2020, the 1099-Misc. has a new sibling, the 1099-NEC, which stands for non-employee compensation. You'll have one or both going out at the end of the year, and it may soon render some of the detail in this chapter obsolete — for example, the 07 box on the 1099-Misc. form no longer functions the way it has in the past. Make sure you get a tutorial from the software company on how to code this new form on their software.

Please see the up-to-date guidelines for the 1099-NEC, and study https://www.irs.gov/forms-pubs/about-form-1099-nec for current information.

Chapter 12

Clerk Work: A/P

(*Accounts Payable*)

What's that you say? Purchase orders and (gasp!) taxes haven't scared you off? All right, then. Let's tackle A/P.

TOOLS:
- Invoices, whether emailed or mailed
- Approval stamp
- PO accordion folder (where you'll house your entered POs and their backups, in alphabetical order)
- Budget
- Cost report (printed from the accounting software each time you code anything)
- All pending POs

We start with the invoices. Alphabetize them, then circle or highlight the fol-

lowing info on each invoice:
- Invoice #
- Invoice date
- Rental periods
- PO # section
- Amount

Remember the approval stamps we looked at in Chapter 10? Stamp all invoices in a clear area and not over the mail-in stub or over text. Fill in the info requested on the stamp. Need a refresher on how that works? It's there for you on page 76.

Double-check your invoices against the good POs, the incomplete PO stack, and any in the accordion folder to make sure nothing's hiding in there that needs to be adjusted. Then fix anything that needs fixing. If you have invoices that don't have matching POs, then you'll need to go to the person who ordered the item. If the invoice doesn't state who requested it, call the vendor and see if they have a contact on file. If they don't, then the detective in you needs to kick in. *Buy a fedora and get to work.*

What department ordered the item? Is it wardrobe, props, set dressing, transportation, locations? Once you narrow that down, contact the department (see your crew list), figure out who made the request, and ask them to come see you so they can a) approve the invoice and b) let you know if this will be the only time they will order from there.

If it won't be, a PO needs to be filled out for the balance of the rental or additional purchases. Then have the purchaser approve the invoice in front of you. Do they have anything else, maybe from a different vendor, coming down the pipeline that they didn't do a PO for? They'll need to request a W-9 or W-8-BEN when they place the order.

Chances are that this is their first show as well and their department head never explained the paperwork part of their job. Let them know that if they have any "loss and damage" at the end of the show, they need to turn in a PO for that as well, with photos of the damaged item and the quote.

Now you should have a good stack, and you should have double-checked if you have POs for each invoice or not. If an invoice is standing solo, no PO, then you only submit the invoice with the approval stamp, making sure you've filled in the boxes. No PO is needed if the INVOICE IS IN YOUR HAND.

If the PO belonging to an invoice has already been entered, then:

A) Attach the PO if the balance on the PO matches the invoice.

B) If the invoice is a draw-down — to be subtracted from the total PO amount — because it was either a rental or a partial payment on a purchase, make a copy of the PO, attach the copy to the invoice, and place the yellow copy back in the accordion file for when the final invoice comes. AND DON'T FORGET TO FILL OUT THE BACK OF THE PO IN THE DRAW-DOWN SECTION FOR THE IN-VOICE IN YOUR HAND (see page 185).

Please use your common sense. If the balance on the PO is less than $50.00, call the vendor and ask if there are any other invoices coming. If not, zero out the balance on the PO and then attach it to the final invoice. Also, make sure the balance in the software is zeroed out.

OK, now that you've matched the A/P to the PO, fill in the stamp with the info it's asking you for. Please make sure you double-check the invoice against the PO. If the PO is not entered, and it's the exact same amount as the invoice, don't enter it. Mark it void and just enter the invoice. If it's a draw-down, make the copy.

This is now ready to put in the "A/P for approval" folder.

Research

The clerk and/or second is usually asked to research items to determine whether they've been paid for, the PO has or hasn't arrived, etc. You may be researching A/P, POs, petty cash, P-cards, or payroll. It's up to you to make sure you know the ins and outs of any software the show is using so you can do this.

Another system is to physically go to the files. If you don't find the item in question, remember it could be in the waiting-to-be-approved, waiting-to-be-scanned, or waiting-to-be-filed pile.

Approvals

The approvals process should happen twice a day, before lunch and again before the end of the day. Usually, by the time lunch rolls around, the folder you dropped off for approval the night before should be ready for you to finish up and you'll have another folder ready for approval, whether it's payroll, petty cash, P-cards, A/P, or POs.

If you have items that are urgent, create an "urgent approval" folder and put that in the accountant's inbox. When you get it back, bring it to the LP or the PM. Check requests are always urgent and need to be turned around ASAP.

Check your office inboxes periodically over the course of the day, and prep your items so you can drop off your evening approval folder for approvals on your way out.

APPROVAL POLY FOLDERS YOU'LL NEED TO MAKE:
CREW PAYROLL FOR APPROVALS
CAST PAYROLL FOR APPROVALS
AP / PO'S FOR APPROVALS
PC AND P-CARDS FOR APPROVALS
URGENT FOR APPROVALS
EXTRAS FOR APPROVALS
A/P CHECKS TO BE SIGNED

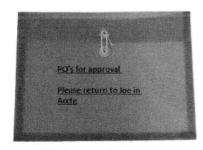

Sample Poly Folder

Note: If this is a long-running show, you'll need to clean up the POs like this every month.

Chapter 13

Letter of Credit

At the start of a production, the accounting department sets up new accounts for all the vendors the production will be working with. As the clerk, you will help to set up these accounts.

On page 106 is an industry-standard credit one-sheet you will use along with the account application to open an account for each new vendor. There are a few vendors that don't even ask for the new account application and only require the one-sheet. The first assistant usually creates this, and I encourage them to teach the clerk and let the clerk help out.

Usually, when a department head begins work on a production, they will give the first assistant a list of vendors they need accounts opened with. That list should be split between the first and you, and you'll call or email all of the vendors on your half of the list to ask for their credit applications. If you're on a studio show, first print out a vendor list from the software. If there's a vendor on the department head's list that you don't see on the software's list, ask your studio financial executive what the protocol is for setting up a new vendor. If you're working with an independent production company, you'll need to call the accounting department at the vendor in question and ask for new account paperwork.

The vendor will have their own form for you to fill out. Every company is different. Along with this, you'll need the production coordinator to send a certificate of insurance (COI) if the vendor is providing a rental or a location – just email the production coordinator letting them know that you've sent the credit application and the vendor needs a COI. To make our lives easier, I always include the production coordinator on the email to the vendor so they're in the loop when setting up a new account.

How will you know if the vendor needs a COI? Trust me. The company will ask for the COI.

The other place that gets a copy of the COI is your payroll company, who in turn gives the production accountant, first, or in-house payroll coordinator one of their COIs for the workers' comp.

SAMPLE CREDIT APPLICATION

CREDIT APPLICATION INFORMATION FOR:

NAME OF PRODUCTIONS, LLC

ASK IF THERE IS A PARENT COMPANY#   DATE

COMPANY NAME   NAME OF PRODUCTIONS, LLC.   FED ID# 00-1234567   1/22/2020

1000 W. Sunset Blvd.

Los Angeles, CA. 90403

PARENT COMPANY   WHOEVER IT IS

1000 W. Sunset Blvd.

Los Angeles, CA. 90403

BANK INFORMATION   CITY NATIONAL BANK   CONTACT: WHOEVER YOUR REP IS

400 ROXBURY DR.   TEL: 310/888-0000

BEVERLY HILLS, CA. 90210

Acct.# 123-456789   NAME ON CHECKING ACCT.

TRADE REFERENCES   WHOEVER YOUR VENDORS ARE

You should list at least four

VIDEO EQUIPMENT RENTAL

912 RUBERTA AVE.   Tel.: 818/956-0000

GLENDALE, CA. 91201   Fax: 818/956-0000

Email:

I authorize my bank to release the following information:

_____

This is for the person who is a signer on the checking account   DATE

Commercial Break

Hi, I'm Courtney. If you're ever looking for someone, just walk on over to craft service. Best place to find people on any show.

Sweet five minutes with my java

Hmmmmm...

Chapter 14

Payroll Coordinator

Let's look ahead for a moment. You've been at this for a little while now, and you've decided which side of production accounting you want to go into. And you choose... payroll! Good choice!

Your first few jobs in payroll should be on non-union shows, or if you do start with SAG-AFTRA straight away, make it a show with a budget of no more than $250,000 in the cast budget line. Do not jump right into working as a payroll coordinator on a huge SAG-AFTRA or IATSE (crew members' union) production. This can be a monster of a job and the stress can be insane. You have to like puzzles and you have to be extremely organized and patient. Once you have worked on several shows, you might be approaching ready. And then it'll be time to buy some software we talked about way back in Chapter 4... Showbiz Timecards.

I DO NOT RECOMMEND STARTING WITH THIS SOFTWARE. You will not get as much out of it as quickly as you would get from doing your first few payrolls manually.

I find that people who start using Showbiz Timecards right off the bat don't become very knowledgeable. Just because they know how to set things up in the software doesn't mean they know the ins and outs of the calculations. It's a shame how many people don't know how to do payroll manually.

If you're not the fastest learner but are interested in working in payroll, you can always take a data entry job at any of the payroll companies and work your way up. But don't be a robot. Make sure you take the initiative to learn and understand as much as you can with the tools the company has.

Since SAG-AFTRA rules can be massive and information heavy, I will touch on them lightly here, and then you should pick up the *Paymaster* book and spend some time on the SAG-AFTRA union website to learn more on your own. At sagaftra.org you can get a wealth of information for free. And there are people out there who hold seminars and classes, so do your homework.

As of April 2018, one resource for learning all things SAG-AFTRA is the class run by a woman named Cecilia Escobar. Her website is www.sasolutionsinc.com. I haven't taken the class myself, so read up on her and check her reviews.

A Little FYI on SAG-AFTRA

Once upon a time, way back before 2012, performers had two unions – SAG and AFTRA. SAG was the Screen Actors Guild, and it covered performers working on episodic shows and feature films. AFTRA was the American Federation of Television and Radio Artists, and in addition to some episodic TV shows (mostly half-hour), it covered variety shows and reality shows.

In March 2012, these two unions merged into the beautiful beast that is SAG-AFTRA. Well, it's beautiful for the performers. For us, it's a little more complicated.

SAG and AFTRA were around as separate entities for donkey's years and old habits die hard in the business, so most of us still refer to the union just as SAG, even though that's no longer its name. Don't correct people when they omit the "AFTRA" bit. It's not a good way to make friends.

On every show, you will be assigned either a SAG or an AFTRA rep. SAG-AFTRA is a musical chairs of contracts and it can all get a bit confusing. You can go to their website and print the blue book for rates and scenarios, and the payroll coordinator or the POC can always call the show's SAG or AFTRA rep. As a clerk, this is not your responsibility.

Working on a SAG-AFTRA Show

TOOLS:
1) Union start packet (if the cast member is just starting)
2) SAG-AFTRA contract: See the deal memo to find out if they are a daily (schedule A) or weekly player (schedule C) or schedule F.
3) Completed Exhibit G: This is the actor's sign-in and sign-out sheet and their work status. From this, you pull the info you need to fill out the actor's time card. You'll also fill out a time sheet for the actors when they do an automated dialogue replacement (ADR) session, usually during post-production. By the time you're doing SAG-AFTRA payroll, you should have a cast payroll Excel sheet, which you'll use to extract the info you need for the time cards: name, Social Security number, company name if the actor has one, tax ID #, and rates.
4) Articles of Incorporation: You'll need a copy if the person is a loan-out.
5) EP *Paymaster* book. You can also go to SAG-AFTRA (http://www.sagaftra.org) to look for the rate sheet.

Let's say one of the actors has just done a single day of ADR. In *The Paymaster*, look up the chapter on SAG-AFTRA, then find the day player contract section and read the ADR information for that type of contract.

INTRO TO PRODUCTION ACCOUNTING

Also, where you fall for a break in the payment method will depend on the budget of the movie. (No idea what I mean? Don't worry — by the time you're working in payroll, it'll make sense!)

A good handful of the forms we've already talked about are part of processing SAG-AFTRA payroll. They need to come back to accounting completed and then be processed for coding and approvals before you submit to either the payroll company or Business Affairs at the studio.

Always, before submitting anything to anyone, double-check your work and make sure the producer or accountant has signed off.

In my experience on episodic shows, most studios process the above-the-line payroll — above-the-line roles are executive producers, producers, writers, directors, and some lead actors. Production Finance or Business Affairs will let you know who will pay these people, the studio or the show, and if you don't hear from them, it's your job to ask.

The completed forms that need to come back to you:
Exhibit G
Union start form
W-4 (if they are an individual)
I-9
W-9 (if they are a loan-out)
Copies of their Articles of Incorporation (if they are a loan-out)
SAG-AFTRA contract (daily, weekly, or long-form)
Check authorization from their agent or manager (if applicable)

Once you have the above, write out the actor's time cards and break them down using the Exhibit Gs you were given (see samples on pages 145–149). Calculate them, code them, and always double-check your work before you submit the complete packet for approvals. And as always, make sure you're doing everything the way your production accountant likes it.

Chapter 15

Hey, It's a Wrap!

When a show wraps, I like for all of the people in my department to dot their i's and cross their t's. *It's nice if they also know the other twenty-four letters of the alphabet.* I have my team build a wrap binder to turn in to the studio, the PFE, the CFO, or our contact person at the production company. This binder contains everything the studio or production company might want to have on file after my team and I have gone.

1) The first assistant or clerk, depending on how much money you have left in your accounting department budget, makes sure all POs in the system are up to date and any that can be voided are removed. (Remember, you can void a PO if you have the complete invoice in hand and there is no outstanding amount still to be invoiced.) Sometimes, you'll have POs with small amounts lingering around, and those can be removed as well. The first/clerk also calls all vendors to make sure there are no outstanding problems and creates a spreadsheet to track what they find. If there are any Loss and Damage items, a PO needs to be submitted and approved by the department head, PM, or LP before they leave.

2) You'll close all PCs. Does the last envelope turned in match the balance on that person's line on the **trial balance**, which tracks who has PC, P-cards, deposit, and A/R? It really, really should. The balance of cash is deposited into the main bank account and the final journal entry is made.

3) The same goes for the P-cards and receipts — before the employees leave the show, they need to turn in all outstanding receipts so accounting can enter them and close down the cards. There will always be some stragglers. You'll have to transfer all the miscellaneous amounts (anything under $5.00) on the software to the P-card custodian, and once you have one consolidated amount, you can request for the card to be closed and a check to be returned or funds to be wired to the production company. When you receive the money, complete the journal entry so the P-card balance is logged as zero.

4) All workers' comp issues are put in the wrap binder (remember, that's the one the PC and the payroll coordinator are building to turn in to the accountant).

5) The payroll coordinator makes a list of anyone they are missing paperwork from and enters a PO into the accounting system with the amounts each person is due, including fringes (estimates are okay).

6) All of these items should be filed and completed as best as possible before everyone leaves.

7) The clerk, and the second assistant if there is one, starts wrapping up the show in boxes once everything is filed away. The boxes should be clearly marked with what they contain, especially the first and last file in each box. Everything should be boxed by item — all A/P files go together, all PC files together, etc.

LABEL SAMPLE:

BOX I
A/P
ABC EQUIPMENT — ECHO SOUND RENTAL

8) You'll make a wrap list of the office items and equipment the department is giving back to the production coordinator. This will include things like "4 desk phones, 2 HP printers," etc.

9) All blank accounting forms get boxed up as well. Keep all of the blank check stock and envelopes in their own box, clearly marked. Send back all leftover payroll forms to the payroll company. Ask your PFE at the studio (or the CFO if it's an independent company) if they need any forms — always recycle when you can!

People tend to scatter like roaches at the end, and it is frustrating when the accounting team needs approvals. So hopefully you've kept on top of everything throughout the production, especially in the final weeks, and you won't need to chase anyone down while they're relaxing on the beach (or already rolling on their next job elsewhere).

Chapter 16

Breaking In

Okay. You've studied the tutorials. You've taken a class or two. And you've read this book cover to cover — at least once. You're ready for your first job!

STEP AWAY FROM LINKEDIN. Sure, you might strike gold on there, but it's not likely unless you're looking for a staff position. You're not joining just any old profession. This is showbusiness. And just as you've always heard, in Hollywood, it's all about that personal connection.

For some reason, a lot of people dread networking. I'm not sure why. Networking doesn't have to be you in a conference center full of intimidatingly accomplished people who don't want to talk to you — anything that gets you meeting and talking to decision makers can count. (*Don't just turn up on their doorsteps, though. That's not a good way to get noticed.*)

And by the way, you may be surprised how many of those intimidating people actually *do* want to talk to you. It's part of why they're in that massive conference room as well.

But the people you meet at events might not be the ones hiring. So how do you find the ones who are?

Well, every payroll company has a marketing department, and there will be several people in that department who are constantly getting calls and emails asking if they know of anyone available and ready to work. You need to make sure those people know of you.

So, pick up the phone and call some marketing departments! Find out who you should send your resume to. While you're there, ask how many people actually call this particular department this way. It never hurts to know the field.

Some people may be rude, so don't be surprised. Just move on to the next person.

Call around to the studios as well and see if you can find out who the production finance department contacts are. Ask who you can speak to if you want to send them your freelance production accounting resume.

Another place to try is the American Film Market (if films are the type of show you want to work on). This huge event happens every November, usually at the Loews Santa Monica Beach Hotel. Go meet people. Everyone hangs out in the lobby, since you need a pass to go into the exhibitors' rooms.

There are several groups on Facebook as well where people share production accounting opportunities:

FILM/TV ACCOUNTANTS AVAILABILITY PAGE:
https://www.facebook.com/groups/1420680558252725/

NY PRODUCTION ACCOUNTANTS:
https://www.facebook.com/groups/143961440154/

ATLANTA PRODUCTION ACCOUNTANTS:

https://www.facebook.com/groups/1462849103971567/

LA PRODUCTION ACCOUNTANTS:
https://www.facebook.com/groups/263105437134632/

You can also take extension classes at UCLA or USC (and you should). They're a great way to meet new people, including the guest speakers, who are generally big players in the field.

Also check out CatchaBreakPodcast.com – "the insider's guide to breaking into and navigating Hollywood."

I'm sure many more avenues are out there. Just do your research and figure it out.

The best for last: Emily Rice has been gracious enough for the last several years to host a blog that lists what producers, companies, and fellow production accountants are looking for:
https://www.ricegortonpictures.com/thelist/

THANK YOU, EMILY, FOR YOUR YEARS OF CONTRIBUTIONS TO US FREELANCERS!

FYI: Most of the studios and bigger companies will do background checks on you. They don't want people stealing their money. *So, make sure you're not a felon.*

Chapter 17

Production Form Examples

At last! It's time to take a look at examples of the forms you've been learning so much about. Every payroll company has their own forms. The ones I'm sharing here are from Media Services, and they're a good baseline for what to expect.

I've also included a purchase order sample, a petty cash cover, and an invoice with an approval stamp on it.

These are really only a few of the forms you'll learn your way around, but they should be enough to make your first few days on the job feel a little less unfamiliar.

What is a W-4?

A W-4 informs your employer how much tax to withhold from each individual paycheck. For further reading, see https://www.irs.gov/forms-instructions.

What is an I-9?

An I-9 form is issued to verify the identity and employment authorization of individuals hired by a company.

A couple thoughts on I-9s:
Two things come up constantly when checking employees' I-9s.

The first is employees often make a mistake on page 2. Employees often write the wrong form of identification in the wrong column. Make sure passports go in column A, driver's licenses go in column B, and Social Security cards go in column C. Also remember, their options are either to fill in column A or to fill in both column B and column C — read the list of acceptable documents that's attached to the I-9 (see page 128).

I know, I know, the last page of the I-9 explains this. Yet another instance of someone overlooking useful information. Get used to that in accounting. Heck, get used to that in life.

The second is employees often forget to sign the bottom of page 1 and forget to check the box "I did not use a preparer or translator."

You should always double- and triple-check employee and actor paperwork, but be extra careful when it comes to these two sections of I-9s. There is a fine if the wrong information — or too much information! — is turned in.

BLANK W-4

Form **W-4**	**Employee's Withholding Certificate**	OMB No. 1545-0074

Department of the Treasury
Internal Revenue Service

► Complete Form W-4 so that your employer can withhold the correct federal income tax from your pay.
► Give Form W-4 to your employer.
► Your withholding is subject to review by the IRS.

2020

Step 1:
Enter
Personal
Information

(a) First name and middle initial   Last name   (b) Social security number

Address

City or town, state, and ZIP code

► Does your name match the name on your social security card? If not, to ensure you get credit for your earnings, contact SSA at 800-772-1213 or go to www.ssa.gov.

(c) ☐ Single or Married filing separately
☐ Married filing jointly (or Qualifying widow(er))
☐ Head of household (Check only if you're unmarried and pay more than half the costs of keeping up a home for yourself and a qualifying individual.)

Complete Steps 2–4 ONLY if they apply to you; otherwise, skip to Step 5. See page 2 for more information on each step, who can claim exemption from withholding, when to use the online estimator, and privacy.

Step 2:
Multiple Jobs
or Spouse
Works

Complete this step if you (1) hold more than one job at a time, or (2) are married filing jointly and your spouse also works. The correct amount of withholding depends on income earned from all of these jobs.

Do **only one** of the following.

(a) Use the estimator at www.irs.gov/W4App for most accurate withholding for this step (and Steps 3–4); **or**

(b) Use the Multiple Jobs Worksheet on page 3 and enter the result in Step 4(c) below for roughly accurate withholding; **or**

(c) If there are only two jobs total, you may check this box. Do the same on Form W-4 for the other job. This option is accurate for jobs with similar pay; otherwise, more tax than necessary may be withheld . . . . . ► ☐

TIP: To be accurate, submit a 2020 Form W-4 for all other jobs. If you (or your spouse) have self-employment income, including as an independent contractor, use the estimator.

Complete Steps 3–4(b) on Form W-4 for only ONE of these jobs. Leave those steps blank for the other jobs. (Your withholding will be most accurate if you complete Steps 3–4(b) on the Form W-4 for the highest paying job.)

Step 3:
Claim
Dependents

If your income will be $200,000 or less ($400,000 or less if married filing jointly):

Multiply the number of qualifying children under age 17 by $2,000 ► $

Multiply the number of other dependents by $500 . . . . ► $

Add the amounts above and enter the total here . . . . | 3 | $

Step 4 (optional):
Other
Adjustments

(a) **Other income (not from jobs).** If you want tax withheld for other income you expect this year that won't have withholding, enter the amount of other income here. This may include interest, dividends, and retirement income . . . . | 4(a) | $

(b) **Deductions.** If you expect to claim deductions other than the standard deduction and want to reduce your withholding, use the Deductions Worksheet on page 3 and enter the result here . . . . | 4(b) | $

(c) **Extra withholding.** Enter any additional tax you want withheld each **pay period** . | 4(c) | $

Step 5:
Sign
Here

Under penalties of perjury, I declare that this certificate, to the best of my knowledge and belief, is true, correct, and complete.

► **Employee's signature** (This form is not valid unless you sign it.)   ► Date

Employers Only

Employer's name and address   First date of employment   Employer identification number (EIN)

For Privacy Act and Paperwork Reduction Act Notice, see page 3.   Cat. No. 10220Q   Form **W-4** (2020)

BLANK W-4 Page 2

General Instructions

Future Developments

For the latest information about developments related to Form W-4, such as legislation enacted after it was published, go to *www.irs.gov/FormW4*.

Purpose of Form

Complete Form W-4 so that your employer can withhold the correct federal income tax from your pay. If too little is withheld, you will generally owe tax when you file your tax return and may owe a penalty. If too much is withheld, you will generally be due a refund. Complete a new Form W-4 when changes to your personal or financial situation would change the entries on the form. For more information on withholding and when you must furnish a new Form W-4, see Pub. 505.

Exemption from withholding. You may claim exemption from withholding for 2020 if you meet both of the following conditions: you had no federal income tax liability in 2019 **and** you expect to have no federal income tax liability in 2020. You had no federal income tax liability in 2019 if (1) your total tax on line 16 on your 2019 Form 1040 or 1040-SR is zero (or less than the sum of lines 18a, 18b, and 18c), or (2) you were not required to file a return because your income was below the filing threshold for your correct filing status. If you claim exemption, you will have no income tax withheld from your paycheck and may owe taxes and penalties when you file your 2020 tax return. To claim exemption from withholding, certify that you meet both of the conditions above by writing "Exempt" on Form W-4 in the space below Step 4(c). Then, complete Steps 1(a), 1(b), and 5. Do not complete any other steps. You will need to submit a new Form W-4 by February 16, 2021.

Your privacy. If you prefer to limit information provided in Steps 2 through 4, use the online estimator, which will also increase accuracy.

As an alternative to the estimator: if you have concerns with Step 2(c), you may choose Step 2(b); if you have concerns with Step 4(a), you may enter an additional amount you want withheld per pay period in Step 4(c). If this is the only job in your household, you may instead check the box in Step 2(c), which will increase your withholding and significantly reduce your paycheck (often by thousands of dollars over the year).

When to use the estimator. Consider using the estimator at *www.irs.gov/W4App* if you:

1. Expect to work only part of the year;

2. Have dividend or capital gain income, or are subject to additional taxes, such as the additional Medicare tax;

3. Have self-employment income (see below); or

4. Prefer the most accurate withholding for multiple job situations.

Self-employment. Generally, you will owe both income and self-employment taxes on any self-employment income you receive separate from the wages you receive as an employee. If you want to pay these taxes through withholding from your wages, use the estimator at *www.irs.gov/W4App* to figure the amount to have withheld.

Nonresident alien. If you're a nonresident alien, see Notice 1392, Supplemental Form W-4 Instructions for Nonresident Aliens, before completing this form.

Specific Instructions

Step 1(c). Check your anticipated filing status. This will determine the standard deduction and tax rates used to compute your withholding.

Step 2. Use this step if you (1) have more than one job at the same time, or (2) are married filing jointly and you and your spouse both work.

Option **(a)** most accurately calculates the additional tax you need to have withheld, while option **(b)** does so with a little less accuracy.

If you (and your spouse) have a total of only two jobs, you may instead check the box in option **(c)**. The box must also be checked on the Form W-4 for the other job. If the box is checked, the standard deduction and tax brackets will be cut in half for each job to calculate withholding. This option is roughly accurate for jobs with similar pay; otherwise, more tax than necessary may be withheld, and this extra amount will be larger the greater the difference in pay is between the two jobs.

 Multiple jobs. *Complete Steps 3 through 4(b) on only one Form W-4. Withholding will be most accurate if you do this on the Form W-4 for the highest paying job.*

Step 3. Step 3 of Form W-4 provides instructions for determining the amount of the child tax credit and the credit for other dependents that you may be able to claim when you file your tax return. To qualify for the child tax credit, the child must be under age 17 as of December 31, must be your dependent who generally lives with you for more than half the year, and must have the required social security number. You may be able to claim a credit for other dependents for whom a child tax credit can't be claimed, such as an older child or a qualifying relative. For additional eligibility requirements for these credits, see Pub. 972, Child Tax Credit and Credit for Other Dependents. You can also include **other tax credits** in this step, such as education tax credits and the foreign tax credit. To do so, add an estimate of the amount for the year to your credits for dependents and enter the total amount in Step 3. Including these credits will increase your paycheck and reduce the amount of any refund you may receive when you file your tax return.

Step 4 (optional).

Step 4(a). Enter in this step the total of your other estimated income for the year, if any. You shouldn't include income from any jobs or self-employment. If you complete Step 4(a), you likely won't have to make estimated tax payments for that income. If you prefer to pay estimated tax rather than having tax on other income withheld from your paycheck, see Form 1040-ES, Estimated Tax for Individuals.

Step 4(b). Enter in this step the amount from the Deductions Worksheet, line 5, if you expect to claim deductions other than the basic standard deduction on your 2020 tax return and want to reduce your withholding to account for these deductions. This includes both itemized deductions and other deductions such as for student loan interest and IRAs.

Step 4(c). Enter in this step any additional tax you want withheld from your pay **each pay period**, including any amounts from the Multiple Jobs Worksheet, line 4. Entering an amount here will reduce your paycheck and will either increase your refund or reduce any amount of tax that you owe.

BLANK W-4 Page 3

Step 2(b)—Multiple Jobs Worksheet *(Keep for your records.)*

If you choose the option in Step 2(b) on Form W-4, complete this worksheet (which calculates the total extra tax for all jobs) on **only ONE** Form W-4. Withholding will be most accurate if you complete the worksheet and enter the result on the Form W-4 for the highest paying job.

Note: If more than one job has annual wages of more than $120,000 or there are more than three jobs, see Pub. 505 for additional tables; or, you can use the online withholding estimator at *www.irs.gov/W4App*.

1   **Two jobs.** If you have two jobs or you're married filing jointly and you and your spouse each have one job, find the amount from the appropriate table on page 4. Using the "Higher Paying Job" row and the "Lower Paying Job" column, find the value at the intersection of the two household salaries and enter that value on line 1. Then, **skip** to line 3 . . . .   **1** $ _____

2   **Three jobs.** If you and/or your spouse have three jobs at the same time, complete lines 2a, 2b, and 2c below. Otherwise, skip to line 3.

    a Find the amount from the appropriate table on page 4 using the annual wages from the highest paying job in the "Higher Paying Job" row and the annual wages for your next highest paying job in the "Lower Paying Job" column. Find the value at the intersection of the two household salaries and enter that value on line 2a . . . .   **2a** $ _____

    b Add the annual wages of the two highest paying jobs from line 2a together and use the total as the wages in the "Higher Paying Job" row and use the annual wages for your third job in the "Lower Paying Job" column to find the amount from the appropriate table on page 4 and enter this amount on line 2b . . . .   **2b** $ _____

    c Add the amounts from lines 2a and 2b and enter the result on line 2c . . . .   **2c** $ _____

3   Enter the number of pay periods per year for the highest paying job. For example, if that job pays weekly, enter 52; if it pays every other week, enter 26; if it pays monthly, enter 12, etc. . . . . .   **3** _____

4   **Divide** the annual amount on line 1 or line 2c by the number of pay periods on line 3. Enter this amount here and in **Step 4(c)** of Form W-4 for the highest paying job (along with any other additional amount you want withheld) . . . .   **4** $ _____

Step 4(b)—Deductions Worksheet *(Keep for your records.)*

1   Enter an estimate of your 2020 itemized deductions (from Schedule A (Form 1040 or 1040-SR)). Such deductions may include qualifying home mortgage interest, charitable contributions, state and local taxes (up to $10,000), and medical expenses in excess of 7.5% of your income . . . .   **1** $ _____

2   Enter: • $24,800 if you're married filing jointly or qualifying widow(er)
            • $18,650 if you're head of household   . . . .   **2** $ _____
            • $12,400 if you're single or married filing separately

3   If line 1 is greater than line 2, subtract line 2 from line 1. If line 2 is greater than line 1, enter "-0-" . .   **3** $ _____

4   Enter an estimate of your student loan interest, deductible IRA contributions, and certain other adjustments (from Part II of Schedule 1 (Form 1040 or 1040-SR)). See Pub. 505 for more information   **4** $ _____

5   **Add** lines 3 and 4. Enter the result here and in **Step 4(b)** of Form W-4 . . . .   **5** $ _____

BLANK W-4 Page 4

Married Filing Jointly or Qualifying Widow(er)

Higher Paying Job Annual Taxable Wage & Salary	\$0 - 9,999	\$10,000 - 19,999	\$20,000 - 29,999	\$30,000 - 39,999	\$40,000 - 49,999	\$50,000 - 59,999	\$60,000 - 69,999	\$70,000 - 79,999	\$80,000 - 89,999	\$90,000 - 99,999	\$100,000 - 109,999	\$110,000 - 120,000
$0 - 9,999	$0	$220	$850	$900	$1,020	$1,020	$1,020	$1,020	$1,020	$1,210	$1,870	$1,870
$10,000 - 19,999	220	1,220	1,900	2,100	2,220	2,220	2,220	2,220	2,410	3,410	4,070	4,070
$20,000 - 29,999	850	1,900	2,730	2,930	3,050	3,050	3,050	3,240	4,240	5,240	5,900	5,900
$30,000 - 39,999	900	2,100	2,930	3,130	3,250	3,250	3,440	4,440	5,440	6,440	7,100	7,100
$40,000 - 49,999	1,020	2,220	3,050	3,250	3,370	3,570	4,570	5,570	6,570	7,570	8,220	8,220
$50,000 - 59,999	1,020	2,220	3,050	3,250	3,570	4,570	5,570	6,570	7,570	8,570	9,220	9,220
$60,000 - 69,999	1,020	2,220	3,050	3,440	4,570	5,570	6,570	7,570	8,570	9,570	10,220	10,220
$70,000 - 79,999	1,020	2,220	3,240	4,440	5,570	6,570	7,570	8,570	9,570	10,570	11,220	11,240
$80,000 - 99,999	1,060	3,260	5,090	6,290	7,420	8,420	9,420	10,420	11,420	12,420	13,260	13,460
$100,000 - 149,999	1,870	4,070	5,900	7,100	8,220	9,320	10,520	11,720	12,920	14,120	14,980	15,180
$150,000 - 239,999	2,040	4,440	6,470	7,870	9,190	10,390	11,590	12,790	13,990	15,190	16,050	16,250
$240,000 - 259,999	2,040	4,440	6,470	7,870	9,190	10,390	11,590	12,790	13,990	15,520	17,170	18,170
$260,000 - 279,999	2,040	4,440	6,470	7,870	9,190	10,390	11,590	13,120	15,120	17,120	18,770	19,770
$280,000 - 299,999	2,040	4,440	6,470	7,870	9,190	10,720	12,720	14,720	16,720	18,720	20,370	21,370
$300,000 - 319,999	2,040	4,440	6,470	8,200	10,320	12,320	14,320	16,320	18,320	20,320	21,970	22,970
$320,000 - 364,999	2,720	5,920	8,750	10,950	13,070	15,070	17,070	19,070	21,290	23,590	25,540	26,840
$365,000 - 524,999	2,970	6,470	9,600	12,100	14,530	16,830	19,130	21,430	23,730	26,030	27,980	29,280
$525,000 and over	3,140	6,840	10,170	12,870	15,500	18,000	20,500	23,000	25,500	28,000	30,150	31,650

Single or Married Filing Separately

Higher Paying Job Annual Taxable Wage & Salary	\$0 - 9,999	\$10,000 - 19,999	\$20,000 - 29,999	\$30,000 - 39,999	\$40,000 - 49,999	\$50,000 - 59,999	\$60,000 - 69,999	\$70,000 - 79,999	\$80,000 - 89,999	\$90,000 - 99,999	\$100,000 - 109,999	\$110,000 - 120,000
$0 - 9,999	$460	$940	$1,020	$1,020	$1,470	$1,870	$1,870	$1,870	$1,870	$2,040	$2,040	$2,040
$10,000 - 19,999	940	1,530	1,610	2,060	3,060	3,460	3,460	3,460	3,640	3,830	3,830	3,830
$20,000 - 29,999	1,020	1,610	2,130	3,130	4,130	4,540	4,540	4,720	4,920	5,110	5,110	5,110
$30,000 - 39,999	1,020	2,060	3,130	4,130	5,130	5,540	5,720	5,920	6,120	6,310	6,310	6,310
$40,000 - 59,999	1,870	3,460	4,540	5,540	6,690	7,290	7,490	7,690	7,890	8,080	8,080	8,080
$60,000 - 79,999	1,870	3,460	4,690	5,890	7,090	7,690	7,890	8,090	8,290	8,480	9,260	10,060
$80,000 - 99,999	2,020	3,810	5,090	6,290	7,490	8,090	8,290	8,490	9,470	10,460	11,260	12,060
$100,000 - 124,999	2,040	3,830	5,110	6,310	7,510	8,430	9,430	10,430	11,430	12,420	13,520	14,620
$125,000 - 149,999	2,040	3,830	5,110	7,030	9,030	10,430	11,430	12,580	13,880	15,170	16,270	17,370
$150,000 - 174,999	2,360	4,950	7,030	9,030	11,030	12,730	14,030	15,330	16,630	17,920	19,020	20,120
$175,000 - 199,999	2,720	5,310	7,540	9,840	12,140	13,840	15,140	16,440	17,740	19,030	20,130	21,230
$200,000 - 249,999	2,970	5,860	8,240	10,540	12,840	14,540	15,840	17,140	18,440	19,730	20,830	21,930
$250,000 - 399,999	2,970	5,860	8,240	10,540	12,840	14,540	15,840	17,140	18,440	19,730	20,830	21,930
$400,000 - 449,999	2,970	5,860	8,240	10,540	12,840	14,540	15,840	17,140	18,450	19,940	21,240	22,540
$450,000 and over	3,140	6,230	8,810	11,310	13,810	15,710	17,210	18,710	20,210	21,700	23,000	24,300

Head of Household

Higher Paying Job Annual Taxable Wage & Salary	\$0 - 9,999	\$10,000 - 19,999	\$20,000 - 29,999	\$30,000 - 39,999	\$40,000 - 49,999	\$50,000 - 59,999	\$60,000 - 69,999	\$70,000 - 79,999	\$80,000 - 89,999	\$90,000 - 99,999	\$100,000 - 109,999	\$110,000 - 120,000
$0 - 9,999	$0	$830	$930	$1,020	$1,020	$1,020	$1,480	$1,870	$1,870	$1,930	$2,040	$2,040
$10,000 - 19,999	830	1,920	2,130	2,220	2,220	2,680	3,680	4,070	4,130	4,330	4,440	4,440
$20,000 - 29,999	930	2,130	2,350	2,430	2,900	3,900	4,900	5,340	5,540	5,740	5,850	5,850
$30,000 - 39,999	1,020	2,220	2,430	2,980	3,980	4,980	6,040	6,630	6,830	7,030	7,140	7,140
$40,000 - 59,999	1,020	2,530	3,750	4,830	5,860	7,060	8,260	8,850	9,050	9,250	9,360	9,360
$60,000 - 79,999	1,870	4,070	5,310	6,600	7,800	9,000	10,200	10,780	10,980	11,180	11,580	12,380
$80,000 - 99,999	1,900	4,300	5,710	7,000	8,200	9,400	10,600	11,180	11,670	12,670	13,580	14,380
$100,000 - 124,999	2,040	4,440	5,850	7,140	8,340	9,540	11,360	12,750	13,750	14,750	15,770	16,870
$125,000 - 149,999	2,040	4,440	5,850	7,360	9,360	11,360	13,360	14,750	16,010	17,310	18,520	19,620
$150,000 - 174,999	2,040	5,060	7,280	9,360	11,360	13,480	15,780	17,460	18,760	20,060	21,270	22,370
$175,000 - 199,999	2,720	5,920	8,130	10,480	12,780	15,080	17,380	19,070	20,370	21,670	22,880	23,980
$200,000 - 249,999	2,970	6,470	8,990	11,370	13,670	15,970	18,270	19,960	21,260	22,560	23,770	24,870
$250,000 - 349,999	2,970	6,470	8,990	11,370	13,670	15,970	18,270	19,960	21,260	22,560	23,770	24,870
$350,000 - 449,999	2,970	6,470	8,990	11,370	13,670	15,970	18,270	19,960	21,260	22,560	23,900	25,200
$450,000 and over	3,140	6,840	9,560	12,140	14,640	17,140	19,640	21,530	23,030	24,530	25,940	27,240

COMPLETED W-4

Form **W-4**	Employee's Withholding Certificate	OMB No. 1545-0074
Department of the Treasury Internal Revenue Service	▶ Complete Form W-4 so that your employer can withhold the correct federal income tax from your pay. ▶ Give Form W-4 to your employer. ▶ Your withholding is subject to review by the IRS.	2020

Step 1: Enter Personal Information

(a) First name and middle initial	Last name	(b) Social security number
JOE Q.	SCHMOE	111-11-1111

Address: 12345 BORING LANE

City or town, state, and ZIP code: CHINATOWN, CA. 99955

▶ Does your name match the name on your social security card? If not, to ensure you get credit for your earnings, contact SSA at 800-772-1213 or go to www.ssa.gov.

(c) ☑ Single or Married filing separately
☐ Married filing jointly (or Qualifying widow(er))
☐ Head of household (Check only if you're unmarried and pay more than half the costs of keeping up a home for yourself and a qualifying individual.)

Complete Steps 2–4 ONLY if they apply to you; otherwise, skip to Step 5. See page 2 for more information on each step, who can claim exemption from withholding, when to use the online estimator, and privacy.

Step 2: Multiple Jobs or Spouse Works

Complete this step if you (1) hold more than one job at a time, or (2) are married filing jointly and your spouse also works. The correct amount of withholding depends on income earned from all of these jobs.

Do **only one** of the following.

(a) Use the estimator at www.irs.gov/W4App for most accurate withholding for this step (and Steps 3–4); **or**

(b) Use the Multiple Jobs Worksheet on page 3 and enter the result in Step 4(c) below for roughly accurate withholding; **or**

(c) If there are only two jobs total, you may check this box. Do the same on Form W-4 for the other job. This option is accurate for jobs with similar pay; otherwise, more tax than necessary may be withheld . . . . . ▶ ☐

TIP: To be accurate, submit a 2020 Form W-4 for all other jobs. If you (or your spouse) have self-employment income, including as an independent contractor, use the estimator.

Complete Steps 3–4(b) on Form W-4 for only ONE of these jobs. Leave those steps blank for the other jobs. (Your withholding will be most accurate if you complete Steps 3–4(b) on the Form W-4 for the highest paying job.)

Step 3: Claim Dependents

If your income will be $200,000 or less ($400,000 or less if married filing jointly):

Multiply the number of qualifying children under age 17 by $2,000 ▶ $ _____

Multiply the number of other dependents by $500 . . . . ▶ $ _____

Add the amounts above and enter the total here . . . . **3** $ _____

Step 4 (optional): Other Adjustments

(a) **Other income (not from jobs).** If you want tax withheld for other income you expect this year that won't have withholding, enter the amount of other income here. This may include interest, dividends, and retirement income . . . . **4(a)** $ _____

(b) **Deductions.** If you expect to claim deductions other than the standard deduction and want to reduce your withholding, use the Deductions Worksheet on page 3 and enter the result here . . . . **4(b)** $ _____

(c) **Extra withholding.** Enter any additional tax you want withheld each **pay period** . **4(c)** $ _____

Step 5: Sign Here

Under penalties of perjury, I declare that this certificate, to the best of my knowledge and belief, is true, correct, and complete.

▶ Employee's signature (This form is not valid unless you sign it.) _____ ▶ Date _____

Employers Only

Employer's name and address	First date of employment	Employer identification number (EIN)
ACCOUNTING IS FUN 4000 MEMORY LANE BURBANK, CA 00000	01/01/2020	95-1111111

For Privacy Act and Paperwork Reduction Act Notice, see page 3. | Cat. No. 10220Q | Form **W-4** (2020)

BLANK I-9

Employment Eligibility Verification
Department of Homeland Security
U.S. Citizenship and Immigration Services

USCIS
Form I-9
OMB No. 1615-0047
Expires 08/31/2019

▶ **START HERE:** Read instructions carefully before completing this form. The instructions must be available, either in paper or electronically, during completion of this form. Employers are liable for errors in the completion of this form.

ANTI-DISCRIMINATION NOTICE: It is illegal to discriminate against work-authorized individuals. Employers **CANNOT** specify which document(s) an employee may present to establish employment authorization and identity. The refusal to hire or continue to employ an individual because the documentation presented has a future expiration date may also constitute illegal discrimination.

Section 1. Employee Information and Attestation *(Employees must complete and sign Section 1 of Form I-9 no later than the first day of employment, but not before accepting a job offer.)*

Last Name *(Family Name)*	First Name *(Given Name)*		Middle Initial	Other Last Names Used *(if any)*	
Address *(Street Number and Name)*		Apt. Number	City or Town	State	ZIP Code
Date of Birth *(mm/dd/yyyy)*	U.S. Social Security Number	Employee's E-mail Address		Employee's Telephone Number	

I am aware that federal law provides for imprisonment and/or fines for false statements or use of false documents in connection with the completion of this form.

I attest, under penalty of perjury, that I am (check one of the following boxes):

☐ 1. A citizen of the United States

☐ 2. A noncitizen national of the United States *(See instructions)*

☐ 3. A lawful permanent resident   (Alien Registration Number/USCIS Number): _____

☐ 4. An alien authorized to work   until (expiration date, if applicable, mm/dd/yyyy): _____
   Some aliens may write "N/A" in the expiration date field. *(See instructions)*

Aliens authorized to work must provide only one of the following document numbers to complete Form I-9:
An Alien Registration Number/USCIS Number OR Form I-94 Admission Number OR Foreign Passport Number.

QR Code - Section 1
Do Not Write In This Space

1. Alien Registration Number/USCIS Number: _____
   OR
2. Form I-94 Admission Number: _____
   OR
3. Foreign Passport Number: _____
   Country of Issuance: _____

Signature of Employee	Today's Date *(mm/dd/yyyy)*

Preparer and/or Translator Certification (check one):
☐ I did not use a preparer or translator.   ☐ A preparer(s) and/or translator(s) assisted the employee in completing Section 1.
(Fields below must be completed and signed when preparers and/or translators assist an employee in completing Section 1.)

I attest, under penalty of perjury, that I have assisted in the completion of Section 1 of this form and that to the best of my knowledge the information is true and correct.

Signature of Preparer or Translator	Today's Date *(mm/dd/yyyy)*	
Last Name *(Family Name)*	First Name *(Given Name)*	
Address *(Street Number and Name)*	City or Town	State	ZIP Code

🛑 *Employer Completes Next Page* 🛑

Form I-9 07/17/17 N

Page 1 of 3

128

BLANK I-9 Page 2

Employment Eligibility Verification
Department of Homeland Security
U.S. Citizenship and Immigration Services

USCIS
Form I-9
OMB No. 1615-0047
Expires 08/31/2019

Section 2. Employer or Authorized Representative Review and Verification

(Employers or their authorized representative must complete and sign Section 2 within 3 business days of the employee's first day of employment. You must physically examine one document from List A OR a combination of one document from List B and one document from List C as listed on the "Lists of Acceptable Documents.")

Employee Info from Section 1	Last Name *(Family Name)*	First Name *(Given Name)*	M.I.	Citizenship/Immigration Status

List A	OR	List B	AND	List C
Identity and Employment Authorization		Identity		Employment Authorization

List A	List B	List C
Document Title	Document Title	Document Title
Issuing Authority	Issuing Authority	Issuing Authority
Document Number	Document Number	Document Number
Expiration Date *(if any)(mm/dd/yyyy)*	Expiration Date *(if any)(mm/dd/yyyy)*	Expiration Date *(if any)(mm/dd/yyyy)*
Document Title		
Issuing Authority	Additional Information	QR Code - Sections 2 & 3 Do Not Write In This Space
Document Number		
Expiration Date *(if any)(mm/dd/yyyy)*		
Document Title		
Issuing Authority		
Document Number		
Expiration Date *(if any)(mm/dd/yyyy)*		

Certification: I attest, under penalty of perjury, that (1) I have examined the document(s) presented by the above-named employee, (2) the above-listed document(s) appear to be genuine and to relate to the employee named, and (3) to the best of my knowledge the employee is authorized to work in the United States.

The employee's first day of employment *(mm/dd/yyyy)*: _____   *(See instructions for exemptions)*

Signature of Employer or Authorized Representative	Today's Date *(mm/dd/yyyy)*	Title of Employer or Authorized Representative
Last Name of Employer or Authorized Representative	First Name of Employer or Authorized Representative	Employer's Business or Organization Name

Employer's Business or Organization Address (Street Number and Name)	City or Town	State	ZIP Code

Section 3. Reverification and Rehires *(To be completed and signed by employer or authorized representative.)*

A. New Name *(if applicable)*			B. Date of Rehire *(if applicable)*
Last Name *(Family Name)*	First Name *(Given Name)*	Middle Initial	Date *(mm/dd/yyyy)*

C. If the employee's previous grant of employment authorization has expired, provide the information for the document or receipt that establishes continuing employment authorization in the space provided below.

Document Title	Document Number	Expiration Date *(if any) (mm/dd/yyyy)*

I attest, under penalty of perjury, that to the best of my knowledge, this employee is authorized to work in the United States, and if the employee presented document(s), the document(s) I have examined appear to be genuine and to relate to the individual.

Signature of Employer or Authorized Representative	Today's Date *(mm/dd/yyyy)*	Name of Employer or Authorized Representative

Form I-9 07/17/17 N

BLANK I-9 Page 3

LISTS OF ACCEPTABLE DOCUMENTS
All documents must be UNEXPIRED

Employees may present one selection from List A
or a combination of one selection from List B and one selection from List C.

LIST A	LIST B	LIST C
Documents that Establish Both Identity and Employment Authorization OR	**Documents that Establish Identity** AND	**Documents that Establish Employment Authorization**
1. U.S. Passport or U.S. Passport Card	1. Driver's license or ID card issued by a State or outlying possession of the United States provided it contains a photograph or information such as name, date of birth, gender, height, eye color, and address	1. A Social Security Account Number card, unless the card includes one of the following restrictions: (1) NOT VALID FOR EMPLOYMENT (2) VALID FOR WORK ONLY WITH INS AUTHORIZATION (3) VALID FOR WORK ONLY WITH DHS AUTHORIZATION
2. Permanent Resident Card or Alien Registration Receipt Card (Form I-551)		
3. Foreign passport that contains a temporary I-551 stamp or temporary I-551 printed notation on a machine-readable immigrant visa	2. ID card issued by federal, state or local government agencies or entities, provided it contains a photograph or information such as name, date of birth, gender, height, eye color, and address	
4. Employment Authorization Document that contains a photograph (Form I-766)	3. School ID card with a photograph	2. Certification of report of birth issued by the Department of State (Forms DS-1350, FS-545, FS-240)
5. For a nonimmigrant alien authorized to work for a specific employer because of his or her status: a. Foreign passport; and b. Form I-94 or Form I-94A that has the following: (1) The same name as the passport; and (2) An endorsement of the alien's nonimmigrant status as long as that period of endorsement has not yet expired and the proposed employment is not in conflict with any restrictions or limitations identified on the form.	4. Voter's registration card 5. U.S. Military card or draft record 6. Military dependent's ID card 7. U.S. Coast Guard Merchant Mariner Card 8. Native American tribal document 9. Driver's license issued by a Canadian government authority **For persons under age 18 who are unable to present a document listed above:**	3. Original or certified copy of birth certificate issued by a State, county, municipal authority, or territory of the United States bearing an official seal 4. Native American tribal document 5. U.S. Citizen ID Card (Form I-197) 6. Identification Card for Use of Resident Citizen in the United States (Form I-179) 7. Employment authorization document issued by the Department of Homeland Security
6. Passport from the Federated States of Micronesia (FSM) or the Republic of the Marshall Islands (RMI) with Form I-94 or Form I-94A indicating nonimmigrant admission under the Compact of Free Association Between the United States and the FSM or RMI	10. School record or report card 11. Clinic, doctor, or hospital record 12. Day-care or nursery school record	

Examples of many of these documents appear in Part 13 of the Handbook for Employers (M-274).

Refer to the instructions for more information about acceptable receipts.

COMPLETED I-9

Employment Eligibility Verification **Department of Homeland Security** U.S. Citizenship and Immigration Services		**USCIS** **Form I-9** OMB No. 1615-0047 Expires 08/31/2019

▶ **START HERE:** Read instructions carefully before completing this form. The instructions must be available, either in paper or electronically, during completion of this form. Employers are liable for errors in the completion of this form.

ANTI-DISCRIMINATION NOTICE: It is illegal to discriminate against work-authorized individuals. Employers **CANNOT** specify which document(s) an employee may present to establish employment authorization and identity. The refusal to hire or continue to employ an individual because the documentation presented has a future expiration date may also constitute illegal discrimination.

Section 1. Employee Information and Attestation *(Employees must complete and sign Section 1 of Form I-9 no later than the **first day of employment**, but not before accepting a job offer.)*

Last Name *(Family Name)* SCHMOE	First Name *(Given Name)* JOE	Middle Initial Q.	Other Last Names Used *(if any)*

Address *(Street Number and Name)* 12345 BORING LANE	Apt. Number	City or Town CHINATOWN	State CA	ZIP Code 99955

Date of Birth *(mm/dd/yyyy)* 1/1/1995	U.S. Social Security Number 1 2 3 - 4 5 - 6 7 8 9	Employee's E-mail Address JOE.SCHMOE.999@GMAIL.COM	Employee's Telephone Number 888-888-8888

I am aware that federal law provides for imprisonment and/or fines for false statements or use of false documents in connection with the completion of this form.

I attest, under penalty of perjury, that I am (check one of the following boxes):

[X] 1. A citizen of the United States

[ ] 2. A noncitizen national of the United States *(See instructions)*

[ ] 3. A lawful permanent resident   (Alien Registration Number/USCIS Number): _____

[ ] 4. An alien authorized to work   until (expiration date, if applicable, mm/dd/yyyy): _____

Some aliens may write "N/A" in the expiration date field. *(See instructions)*

Aliens authorized to work must provide only one of the following document numbers to complete Form I-9:
An Alien Registration Number/USCIS Number OR Form I-94 Admission Number OR Foreign Passport Number.

1. Alien Registration Number/USCIS Number: _____

OR

2. Form I-94 Admission Number: _____

OR

3. Foreign Passport Number: _____

Country of Issuance: _____

QR Code - Section 1
Do Not Write In This Space

Signature of Employee Joe Schmoe's Signature	Today's Date *(mm/dd/yyyy)* 11/01/2019

Preparer and/or Translator Certification (check one):

[X] I did not use a preparer or translator.   [ ] A preparer(s) and/or translator(s) assisted the employee in completing Section 1.

(Fields below must be completed and signed when preparers and/or translators assist an employee in completing Section 1.)

I attest, under penalty of perjury, that I have assisted in the completion of Section 1 of this form and that to the best of my knowledge the information is true and correct.

Signature of Preparer or Translator	Today's Date *(mm/dd/yyyy)*

Last Name *(Family Name)*	First Name *(Given Name)*

Address *(Street Number and Name)*	City or Town	State	ZIP Code

🛑 *Employer Completes Next Page* 🛑

Form I-9 07/17/17 N

Page 1 of 3

131

COMPLETED I-9 Page 2

Employment Eligibility Verification
Department of Homeland Security
U.S. Citizenship and Immigration Services

USCIS
Form I-9
OMB No. 1615-0047
Expires 08/31/2019

Section 2. Employer or Authorized Representative Review and Verification

(Employers or their authorized representative must complete and sign Section 2 within 3 business days of the employee's first day of employment. You must physically examine one document from List A OR a combination of one document from List B and one document from List C as listed on the "Lists of Acceptable Documents.")

Employee Info from Section 1	Last Name *(Family Name)* Schmoe	First Name *(Given Name)* Joe	M.I. Q	Citizenship/Immigration Status 1

List A — Identity and Employment Authorization	OR	List B — Identity	AND	List C — Employment Authorization
Document Title US PASSPORT		Document Title		Document Title
Issuing Authority US DEPT OF STATE		Issuing Authority		Issuing Authority
Document Number 123456789		Document Number		Document Number
Expiration Date *(if any)(mm/dd/yyyy)* 1/1/3020		Expiration Date *(if any)(mm/dd/yyyy)*		Expiration Date *(if any)(mm/dd/yyyy)*
Document Title		Additional Information		QR Code - Sections 2 & 3 Do Not Write In This Space
Issuing Authority				
Document Number				
Expiration Date *(if any)(mm/dd/yyyy)*				
Document Title				
Issuing Authority				
Document Number				
Expiration Date *(if any)(mm/dd/yyyy)*				

Certification: I attest, under penalty of perjury, that (1) I have examined the document(s) presented by the above-named employee, (2) the above-listed document(s) appear to be genuine and to relate to the employee named, and (3) to the best of my knowledge the employee is authorized to work in the United States.

The employee's first day of employment *(mm/dd/yyyy):*   11/03/2019   *(See instructions for exemptions)*

Signature of Employer or Authorized Representative Very Ugly Signature	Today's Date *(mm/dd/yyyy)* 11/01/2019	Title of Employer or Authorized Representative Unit Production Manager
Last Name of Employer or Authorized Representative Organizer	First Name of Employer or Authorized Representative Savvy	Employer's Business or Organization Name Accounting Rocks, LLC

Employer's Business or Organization Address (Street Number and Name) 54321 Exciting Drive	City or Town Happyland	State CA	ZIP Code 99992

Section 3. Reverification and Rehires *(To be completed and signed by employer or authorized representative.)*

A. New Name *(if applicable)*			B. Date of Rehire *(if applicable)*
Last Name *(Family Name)*	First Name *(Given Name)*	Middle Initial	Date *(mm/dd/yyyy)*

C. If the employee's previous grant of employment authorization has expired, provide the information for the document or receipt that establishes continuing employment authorization in the space provided below.

Document Title	Document Number	Expiration Date *(if any) (mm/dd/yyyy)*

I attest, under penalty of perjury, that to the best of my knowledge, this employee is authorized to work in the United States, and if the employee presented document(s), the document(s) I have examined appear to be genuine and to relate to the individual.

Signature of Employer or Authorized Representative	Today's Date *(mm/dd/yyyy)*	Name of Employer or Authorized Representative

Form I-9 07/17/17 N

Page 2 of 3

BLANK NON-UNION START FORM

NON UNION START / CLOSE

PROD. COMPANY			PROD. TITLE			UNION NO.	OCCUP. CODE & SCHEDULE

EMPLOYEE NAME		SOCIAL SECURITY NUMBER	HIRE DATE	START DATE	JOB CLASS	SEX M F O O

EMPLOYEE ADDRESS

CHECK ONE:
○ DAILY EMPLOYEE   ○ WEEKLY EMPLOYEE

CITY

AFFORDABLE CARE ACT EMPLOYMENT BASIS *(MUST CHECK ONE)*:
☐ FULL TIME ☐ PART TIME ☐ VARIABLE HOUR ☐ SEASONAL

STATE	ZIP CODE	PHONE	TERMS OF EMPLOYMENT	STUDIO	LOCATION
E-MAIL ADDRESS			RATE PER HOUR ACCOUNT:		
NAME OF LOANOUT COMPANY			RATE PER WEEK ACCOUNT: OVERTIME RATE IF DIFFERENT FROM GUAR.		
FEDERAL I.D. #	STATE I.D. #		ACCOUNT:		

		TOTAL HOURS*	DAY	WEEK	DAY	WEEK

IS LOANOUT REGISTERED TO DO BUSINESS IN THE STATE IN WHICH FILM IS BEING PRODUCED: ○ YES   ○ NO

IF NO TO ABOVE, IN WHICH STATE ARE YOU REGISTERED:

IF RATE DOES NOT INCLUDE IDLE: ///// PAY SATURDAY $ ///// PAY SUNDAY $

OTHER TERMS & CONDITIONS:

**CAR RENTAL
ACCOUNT:
**MISCELLANEOUS RENTAL
ACCOUNT:
PER DIEM /////
ACCOUNT:

*WHEN APPLICABLE, TOTAL HOURS MAY INCLUDE HOURS RECOGNIZED AS WORK TIME. EMPLOYEES WILL HOLD THEMSELVES IN READINESS TO SERVE THE PRODUCER DURING SUCH TIME.

**THESE ITEMS ARE CONSIDERED TAXABLE INCOME UNLESS A WEEKLY, ITEMIZED INVOICE IS PROVIDED

AS A CONDITION OF EMPLOYMENT, EMPLOYEE AUTHORIZES PRODUCTION COMPANY OR ITS DESIGNEE TO AUTOMATICALLY DEDUCT FROM EMPLOYEE'S PAYCHECK ANY OVERPAYMENTS OR CASH ADVANCES UNACCOUNTED FOR.

EMPLOYEE SIGNATURE	PRODUCTION MANAGEMENT
X	X

BOX/KIT RENTAL AGREEMENT

AS OF JULY 1990, IRS REGULATIONS REQUIRE THAT AN ITEMIZED FORM BE SUBMITTED TO SUBSTANTIATE KIT RENTALS. IF RENTALS ARE NOT SUBSTANTIATED, KIT RENTALS WILL BE SUBJECT TO WITHHOLDING TAXES AT THE SAME RATES AS WAGES.

RENTAL COMMENCES ON: _____ RATE: _____ PER WK

ITEMIZED INVENTORY:

QUANTITY	DESCRIPTION	ITEM VALUE	UNIT RENTAL PRICE

NOTE: IF YOU NEED MORE ROOM, PLEASE ATTACH A SEPARATE SHEET.   TOTAL VALUES:

I ATTEST THAT THE ABOVE DESCRIBED EQUIPMENT REPRESENTS A VALID RENTAL FOR THIS PRODUCTION.

EMPLOYEE SIGNATURE	DATE	APPROVAL SIGNATURE	DATE

Reprint courtesy of Media Services Payroll

COMPLETED NON-UNION START FORM

NON UNION START / CLOSE

PROD. COMPANY			PROD. TITLE			UNION NO	OCCUP CODE & SCHEDULE	
Accounting Rocks, LLC			Production Accounting: The Movie			N/A	1208	
EMPLOYEE NAME			SOCIAL SECURITY NUMBER	HIRE DATE	START DATE	JOB CLASS		SEX
Joe Schmoe			123-45-6789	11/02	11/03	Assistant Accountant		M F ◉ ○

EMPLOYEE ADDRESS		DATE OF BIRTH:		CHECK ONE:	
12345 Boring Lane		01/01/1995		○ DAILY EMPLOYEE	◉ WEEKLY EMPLOYEE

CITY			AFFORDABLE CARE ACT EMPLOYMENT BASIS (MUST CHECK ONE):		
Chinatown			☐ FULL TIME ☐ PART TIME		

STATE	ZIP CODE	PHONE	TERMS OF EMPLOYMENT	STUDIO	LOCATION
CA	99955	888-888-8888	RATE PER HOUR	$0.0714	$0.0714
E-MAIL ADDRESS			ACCOUNT:		
joe.schmoe.999@gmail.com			RATE PER WEEK		
NAME OF LOANOUT COMPANY			ACCOUNT:		
N/A			OVERTIME RATE IF DIFFERENT FROM GUAR.		
FEDERAL I.D. #		STATE I.D. #	ACCOUNT:		

		TOTAL HOURS*	DAY 12		WEEK	DAY 12		WEEK
IS LOANOUT REGISTERED TO DO BUSINESS IN THE STATE IN WHICH FILM IS BEING PRODUCED. ○ YES ○ NO		IF RATE DOES NOT INCLUDE IDLE:	/////	PAY SATURDAY $		PAY SUNDAY $		
IF NO TO ABOVE, IN WHICH STATE ARE YOU REGISTERED		**CAR RENTAL						
OTHER TERMS & CONDITIONS:		ACCOUNT:						
		**MISCELLANEOUS RENTAL						
		ACCOUNT:						
		PER DIEM						
		ACCOUNT:	/////					

*WHEN APPLICABLE, TOTAL HOURS MAY INCLUDE HOURS RECOGNIZED AS WORK TIME. EMPLOYEES WILL HOLD THEMSELVES IN READINESS TO SERVE THE PRODUCER DURING SUCH TIME.

**THESE ITEMS ARE CONSIDERED TAXABLE INCOME UNLESS A WEEKLY, ITEMIZED INVOICE IS PROVIDED

AS A CONDITION OF EMPLOYMENT, EMPLOYEE AUTHORIZES PRODUCTION COMPANY OR ITS DESIGNEE TO AUTOMATICALLY DEDUCT FROM EMPLOYEE'S PAYCHECK ANY OVERPAYMENTS OR CASH ADVANCES UNACCOUNTED FOR.

EMPLOYEE SIGNATURE	PRODUCTION MANAGEMENT
x Joe Schmoe's Signature	x UPM/Line Producer Signature

BOX/KIT RENTAL AGREEMENT

AS OF JULY 1990, IRS REGULATIONS REQUIRE THAT AN ITEMIZED FORM BE SUBMITTED TO SUBSTANTIATE KIT RENTALS. IF RENTALS ARE NOT SUBSTANTIATED, KIT RENTALS WILL BE SUBJECT TO WITHHOLDING TAXES AT THE SAME RATES AS WAGES.

RENTAL COMMENCES ON: 11/03/19   RATE: $50   PER WK

ITEMIZED INVENTORY:

QUANTITY	DESCRIPTION	ITEM VALUE	UNIT RENTAL PRICE
1	Laptop	$1,500	$5
1	Sandwich Maker	$50	$5

NOTE: IF YOU NEED MORE ROOM, PLEASE ATTACH A SEPARATE SHEET.   TOTAL VALUES: $1,550

I ATTEST THAT THE ABOVE DESCRIBED EQUIPMENT REPRESENTS A VALID RENTAL FOR THIS PRODUCTION.

EMPLOYEE SIGNATURE	DATE	APPROVAL SIGNATURE	DATE
Joe Schmoe's Signature	11/01/19	UPM/Line Producer Signature	11/01/19

Reprint courtesy of Media Services Payroll

BLANK UNION START FORM

UNION START / CLOSE

PROD. COMPANY			PROD. TITLE				UNION NO.	OCCUP. CODE & SCHEDULE	
EMPLOYEE NAME			SOCIAL SECURITY NUMBER		HIRE DATE	START DATE	JOB CLASS		SEX M F ○ ○

EMPLOYEE ADDRESS			DATE OF BIRTH:	CHECK ONE: ○ DAILY EMPLOYEE	○ WEEKLY EMPLOYEE

CITY			AFFORDABLE CARE ACT EMPLOYMENT BASIS (MUST CHECK ONE): ☐ FULL TIME ☐ PART TIME

STATE	ZIP CODE	PHONE	TERMS OF EMPLOYMENT	STUDIO	LOCATION
E-MAIL ADDRESS			RATE PER HOUR ACCOUNT:		
NAME OF LOANOUT COMPANY			RATE PER WEEK ACCOUNT:		
FEDERAL I.D. #		STATE I.D. #	OVERTIME RATE IF DIFFERENT FROM GUAR. ACCOUNT:		

	DAY	WEEK	DAY	WEEK
GUARANTEED HOURS				

IS LOANOUT REGISTERED TO DO BUSINESS IN THE STATE IN WHICH FILM IS BEING PRODUCED. ○ YES ○ NO

IF RATE DOES NOT INCLUDE IDLE:		PAY SATURDAY $	PAY SUNDAY $

IF NO TO ABOVE. IN WHICH STATE ARE YOU REGISTERED.

OTHER TERMS & CONDITIONS:

**CAR RENTAL ACCOUNT:	
**MISCELLANEOUS RENTAL	
ACCOUNT:	
PER DIEM	
ACCOUNT:	

**THESE ITEMS ARE CONSIDERED TAXABLE INCOME UNLESS A WEEKLY, ITEMIZED INVOICE IS PROVIDED

AS A CONDITION OF EMPLOYMENT, EMPLOYEE AUTHORIZES PRODUCTION COMPANY OR ITS DESIGNEE TO AUTOMATICALLY DEDUCT FROM EMPLOYEE'S PAYCHECK ANY OVERPAYMENTS OR CASH ADVANCES UNACCOUNTED FOR.

EMPLOYEE SIGNATURE	PRODUCTION MANAGEMENT
X	X

BOX/KIT RENTAL AGREEMENT

AS OF JULY 1990, IRS REGULATIONS REQUIRE THAT AN ITEMIZED FORM BE SUBMITTED TO SUBSTANTIATE KIT RENTALS. IF RENTALS ARE NOT SUBSTANTIATED, KIT RENTALS WILL BE SUBJECT TO WITHHOLDING TAXES AT THE SAME RATES AS WAGES.

RENTAL COMMENCES ON: _____   RATE: _____ PER WK

ITEMIZED INVENTORY:

QUANTITY	DESCRIPTION	ITEM VALUE	UNIT RENTAL PRICE

NOTE. IF YOU NEED MORE ROOM, PLEASE ATTACH A SEPARATE SHEET.   TOTAL VALUES:

I ATTEST THAT THE ABOVE DESCRIBED EQUIPMENT REPRESENTS A VALID RENTAL FOR THIS PRODUCTION.

EMPLOYEE SIGNATURE	DATE	APPROVAL SIGNATURE	DATE

Reprint courtesy of Media Services Payroll

COMPLETED UNION START FORM

UNION START / CLOSE

PROD. COMPANY	PROD. TITLE		UNION NO.	OCCUP. CODE & SCHEDULE
Accounting Rocks, LLC	Production Accounting: The Movie		00000001	1208

EMPLOYEE NAME	SOCIAL SECURITY NUMBER	HIRE DATE	START DATE	JOB CLASS	SEX
Joe Schmoe	123-45-6789	11/02	11/03	Assistant Accountant	M ◉ F ○

EMPLOYEE ADDRESS	DATE OF BIRTH:	CHECK ONE:
12345 Boring Lane	01/01/1995	○ DAILY EMPLOYEE ◉ WEEKLY EMPLOYEE

CITY	AFFORDABLE CARE ACT EMPLOYMENT BASIS (MUST CHECK ONE):
Chinatown	☐ FULL TIME ☐ PART TIME

STATE	ZIP CODE	PHONE	TERMS OF EMPLOYMENT	STUDIO	LOCATION
CA	99955	888-888-8888	RATE PER HOUR	$0.0714	$0.0714
E-MAIL ADDRESS			ACCOUNT:		
joe.schmoe.999@gmail.com			RATE PER WEEK		
NAME OF LOANOUT COMPANY			ACCOUNT:		
N/A			OVERTIME RATE IF DIFFERENT FROM GUAR.		
FEDERAL I.D. #		STATE I.D. #	ACCOUNT:		
			GUARANTEED HOURS	DAY 12	WEEK DAY 12 WEEK
IS LOANOUT REGISTERED TO DO BUSINESS IN THE STATE IN WHICH FILM IS BEING PRODUCED: ○ YES ○ NO			IF RATE DOES NOT INCLUDE IDLE:		PAY SATURDAY $ PAY SUNDAY $
IF NO TO ABOVE, IN WHICH STATE ARE YOU REGISTERED:			**CAR RENTAL		
OTHER TERMS & CONDITIONS:			ACCOUNT:		
			**MISCELLANEOUS RENTAL		
			ACCOUNT:		
			PER DIEM		
			ACCOUNT:		

**THESE ITEMS ARE CONSIDERED TAXABLE INCOME UNLESS A WEEKLY, ITEMIZED INVOICE IS PROVIDED

AS A CONDITION OF EMPLOYMENT, EMPLOYEE AUTHORIZES PRODUCTION COMPANY OR ITS DESIGNEE TO AUTOMATICALLY DEDUCT FROM EMPLOYEE'S PAYCHECK ANY OVERPAYMENTS OR CASH ADVANCES UNACCOUNTED FOR.

EMPLOYEE SIGNATURE	PRODUCTION MANAGEMENT
x Joe Schmoe's Signature	x UPM/Line Producer Signature

BOX/KIT RENTAL AGREEMENT

AS OF JULY 1990, IRS REGULATIONS REQUIRE THAT AN ITEMIZED FORM BE SUBMITTED TO SUBSTANTIATE KIT RENTALS. IF RENTALS ARE NOT SUBSTANTIATED, KIT RENTALS WILL BE SUBJECT TO WITHHOLDING TAXES AT THE SAME RATES AS WAGES.

RENTAL COMMENCES ON: 11/03/19   RATE: $50   PER WK

ITEMIZED INVENTORY:

QUANTITY	DESCRIPTION	ITEM VALUE	UNIT RENTAL PRICE
1	Laptop	$1,500	$5
1	Sandwich Maker	$50	$5

NOTE: IF YOU NEED MORE ROOM, PLEASE ATTACH A SEPARATE SHEET.   TOTAL VALUES: $1,550

I ATTEST THAT THE ABOVE DESCRIBED EQUIPMENT REPRESENTS A VALID RENTAL FOR THIS PRODUCTION.

EMPLOYEE SIGNATURE	DATE	APPROVAL SIGNATURE	DATE
Joe Schmoe's Signature	11/01/19	UPM/Line Producer Signature	11/01/19

Reprint courtesy of Media Services Payroll

BLANK BOX RENTAL FORM

BOX / KIT RENTAL AGREEMENT

NAME: _____ DATE:_____

SOCIAL SECURITY #: _____

JOB NAME / NUMBER: _____

Date	Quantity	Description	Unit Price	Amount

Total Rental Amount: $_____

Employee Signature: _____

Authorized By: _____

Reprint courtesy of Media Services Payroll

COMPLETED BOX RENTAL FORM

BOX / KIT RENTAL AGREEMENT

NAME: JOE SCHMOE   DATE: 11/3/2019

SOCIAL SECURITY #: 123-45-6789

JOB NAME / NUMBER: Assistant Accountant

Date	Quantity	Description	Unit Price	Amount
11/3/2019	1	Laptop	$1,500	$5
11/3/2019	1	Sandwich Maker	$50	$5

Total Rental Amount: $ $10

Employee Signature: Joe Schmoe's Signature

Authorized By: UPM/Line Producer's Signature

Reprint courtesy of Media Services Payroll

BLANK DIRECT DEPOSIT FORM

FREELANCER ACH DEPOSIT
AUTHORIZATION AGREEMENT
FOR AUTOMATIC PAYROLL DEPOSIT PROGRAM

◉ New Agreement   ○ Change Account   ○ Cancel Agreement

The undersigned hereby authorizes the payroll companies managed by Media Services to make automatic payroll deposits to the undersigned's bank account(s) as designated below.

The undersigned acknowledges and agrees that such automatic payroll deposits may be made only if their designated financial institution is a Participating Depository Financial Institution in the Automated Clearing House system.

The ACH payments can only be made on your behalf once your production company employer has funded the payroll so that the payroll company can proceed with finalization. Once the payroll company finalizes the payroll, the ACH deposit will transfer to your account **2 business days after the finalization date**.

The undersigned agrees that if he or she closes the below-named bank account, or elects to terminate their participation in the Automatic Payroll Deposit Program, the undersigned shall immediately notify the payroll company by completing and delivering a new ACH Deposit Authorization Agreement. If the undersigned fails to notify the payroll company of a closed bank account or their termination in the Automatic Payroll Deposit Program, payroll company shall not be liable for deposits directed to the bank account(s) designated below.

Please note that if you work for a production company employer that participates in the Direct Deposit Program, you must switch to Direct Deposit for that production. A Direct Deposit election supersedes ACH.

Please note: By default, your payslip will no longer be printed and mailed, but will be available to you online. **If you require that we continue to print your payslip, please check this box:** ☐

Employee Name (print): _____   Last 4 of SSN: _____
Employee Email: _____
Employee Phone: _____

Employee Signature: _____   Date : _____

Select One: ◉ Checking Account ○ Savings Account ○ Percentage: ___% ○ Amount $ _____
Financial Institution: _____
Account Name: _____   Account No. _____
Routing No: _____
(See check example next page. Do not use a deposit slip.)

Select One: ○ Checking Account ○ Savings Account ○ Percentage: ___% ○ Amount:$ _____
Financial Institution: _____
Account Name: _____   Account No. _____
Routing No. _____

Email completed forms to:

COMPLETED DIRECT DEPOSIT FORM

FREELANCER ACH DEPOSIT
AUTHORIZATION AGREEMENT
FOR AUTOMATIC PAYROLL DEPOSIT PROGRAM

⦿ New Agreement   ○ Change Account   ○ Cancel Agreement

The undersigned hereby authorizes the payroll companies managed by Media Services to make automatic payroll deposits to the undersigned's bank account(s) as designated below.

The undersigned acknowledges and agrees that such automatic payroll deposits may be made only if their designated financial institution is a Participating Depository Financial Institution in the Automated Clearing House system.

The ACH payments can only be made on your behalf once your production company employer has funded the payroll so that the payroll company can proceed with finalization. Once the payroll company finalizes the payroll, the ACH deposit will transfer to your account **2 business days after the finalization date.**

The undersigned agrees that if he or she closes the below-named bank account, or elects to terminate their participation in the Automatic Payroll Deposit Program, the undersigned shall immediately notify the payroll company by completing and delivering a new ACH Deposit Authorization Agreement. If the undersigned fails to notify the payroll company of a closed bank account or their termination in the Automatic Payroll Deposit Program, payroll company shall not be liable for deposits directed to the bank account(s) designated below.

Please note that if you work for a production company employer that participates in the Direct Deposit Program, you must switch to Direct Deposit for that production. A Direct Deposit election supersedes ACH.

Please note: By default, your payslip will no longer be printed and mailed, but will be available to you online. **If you require that we continue to print your payslip, please check this box:** ☐

Employee Name (print): Joe Schmoe   Last 4 of SSN: 6789
Employee Email: joe.schmoe.999@gmail.com
Employee Phone: 818-867-5309

Employee Signature: Joe Schmoe's Signature   Date: 10/25

Select One: ⦿ Checking Account ○ Savings Account ○ Percentage: ____% ○ Amount $ _____
Financial Institution: Bank Of Schmoes
Account Name: Joe Schmoe   Account No. 98124890
Routing No: 2490289048902
(See check example next page. Do not use a deposit slip.)

Select One: ○ Checking Account ○ Savings Account ○ Percentage: ____% ○ Amount: $ _____
Financial Institution: _____
Account Name: _____   Account No. _____
Routing No. _____

Email completed forms to:

Reprint courtesy of Media Services Payroll

BLANK NON-UNION CREW TIME CARD

NON-UNION

Employee Name					Social Security No.						Week Ending						
Loan-Out Corporation					Federal I.D. No.						**WORK LOCATION REQUIRED** Location City _____ County _____						
Production Name					Job Classification						Work State _____ Foreign ☐						
Production Company					Rate						Account Code						

Date	Location Zip Code	1st Meal		2nd Meal			Wrap	Hrs	MP	Acct	St	1½	2	2½	MP		Hrs	Rate	Total
		In	Out	In	Out	In													
Sun									1										
									2						St				
Mon									1										
									2						1½				
Tue									1										
									2						2				
Wed									1										
									2						2½				
Thu									1										
									2										
Fri									1										
									2						MP				
Sat									1										
									2						VAC				

Employee Health Insurance Deduction: $ _____	Special Unpaid Leave:			HOL	
Employment Ended: ☐ No ☐ Yes Date: _____	From _____ To _____				
Comments/Reason For Late Payroll Submission:				ADJ	

ACCT. #	MEALS ALLOWED	MEALS TAXABLE	PER DIEM ADVANCE	ACCT. #	LODGING ALLOW	LODGING TAXABLE	PER DIEM ADVANCE
ACCT. #	BOX RENTAL	ACCT. #	CAR ALLOW	ACCT. #	MILEAGE ALLOW	MILEAGE TAXABLE	MILEAGE ADVANCE
CHECK ONE: ☐ BOX RENTAL INFORMATION ON FILE ☐ BOX RENTAL INFORMATION ATTACHED				ACCT. #	2ND CAMERA	OTHER	SALARY ADVANCE
COMMENTS:						**Total $**	

BY SIGNING, YOU CERTIFY THAT THE RECORD OF TIME WORKED IS CORRECT. WITHOUT APPROPRIATE DOCUMENTATION, REIMBURSABLE EXPENSES WILL BE CONSIDERED TAXABLE ITEMS.

EMPLOYEE
SIGNATURE X _____ APPROVED X _____

Reprint courtesy of Media Services Payroll

A couple notes about this time card:

Joe Schmoe worked one full day, so, based on the box rental form we looked at earlier, he receives $10 for his box rental.

To avoid being taxed for his mileage reimbursement, Joe Schmoe must fill out an itemized mileage sheet, which needs to be turned in with his time card.

If the show gives employees per diem, go to the link on page 142 to see what is taxable and the amount that is not taxable by the state and city you are working in.

COMPLETED NON-UNION CREW TIME CARD

NON-UNION

							Week Ending			11/09			
Employee Name Joe Schmoe				Social Security No. 123-45-6789				**WORK LOCATION REQUIRED**					
Loan-Out Corporation N/A				Federal I.D. No. N/A				Location City			County		
								Work State			Foreign ☐		
Production Name Production Accounting: The Movie				Job Classification Asst. Accountant									
Production Company Accounting Rocks, LLC				Rate $1/day				Account Code 1208					

			1st Meal		2nd Meal							**For Accounting Use Only**						
Date	Location Zip Code	In	Out	In	Out	In	Wrap	Hrs	MP	Acct	St	1½	2	2½	MP	Hrs	Rate	Total
Sun 11/03	99999	9.0	15.0	15.5			21.5	12.0	1 2		8	4			St	8	.0714	.5714
Mon 11/04	TRAVEL								1 2						1½	4	.1071	.4286
Tue 11/05									1 2					2				
Wed 11/06									1 2					2½				
Thu 11/07									1 2									
Fri 11/08									1 2						MP			
Sat 11/09									1 2						VAC			

Employee Health Insurance Deduction: $ _____	Special Unpaid Leave:	HOL
Employment Ended: ☐ No ☑ Yes Date: _____	From ____ To ____	
Comments/Reason For Late Payroll Submission: 1 Day Per Diem $30/day. 1 Day Box Rental $10/day. 11/4 Travel Day - 1/2 Day Pay. $15 Meal Stipend on Travel Day		ADJ

ACCT # 1215	MEALS ALLOWED $15	MEALS TAXABLE N/A	PER DIEM ADVANCE $30	ACCT # N/A	LODGING ALLOW N/A	LODGING TAXABLE N/A	PER DIEM ADVANCE N/A
ACCT # 1209	BOX RENTAL $10/day	ACCT # 3540	CAR ALLOW $67.89	ACCT # N/A	MILEAGE ALLOW N/A	MILEAGE TAXABLE N/A	MILEAGE ADVANCE N/A
CHECK ONE:	☑ BOX RENTAL INFORMATION ON FILE ☐ BOX RENTAL INFORMATION ATTACHED			ACCT # N/A	2ND CAMERA N/A	OTHER N/A	SALARY ADVANCE N/A

CA personnel: We have a Medical Provider Network (MPN) for all work-related injuries and/or illnesses. In the event of an injury, your care will be directed to a physician within the MPN. You may qualify to pre-designate a doctor. For more information, please contact us at 310 440 9675 or wcdapt@media-services.com.

Total $ 124.39

BY SIGNING, YOU CERTIFY THAT THE RECORD OF TIME WORKED IS CORRECT. WITHOUT APPROPRIATE DOCUMENTATION, REIMBURSABLE EXPENSES WILL BE CONSIDERED TAXABLE ITEMS.

EMPLOYEE SIGNATURE X _____ Joe Schmoe's Signature _____   APPROVED X _____ UPM/Line Producer's Signature _____

Reprint courtesy of Media Services Payroll

The US General Service Administration breaks down the rules on per diem in detail. You can go to this link for their list of per diem rates around the world: https://www.gsa.gov/travel/plan-book/per-diem-rates/

Joe worked one full day on location, therefore he received $30 per diem. Since his travel was only a half day, production didn't pay per diem for it.

For meals, per diem, box rentals, and car allowance, look at the budget and find the correct codes. I've mentioned this before, but it bears repeating: read the budget as thoroughly as possible before starting a shoot. It will make this process much quicker. For doing payroll, write a cheat sheet

BLANK UNION CREW TIME CARD

UNION

										Week Ending		
Employee Name				Social Security No.						**WORK LOCATION REQUIRED**		
Loan-Out Corporation				Federal I.D. No.						Location City ___ County ___ Work State ___ Foreign ☐		
Production Name				Job Classification		Union No.				Union Occupation Code and Schedule		
Production Company				Rate		Guar. Hrs.				Account Code		

Date	Location Zip Code	In	Out	In	Out	In	Wrap	Hrs	MP	Acct	St	1½	2	2½	MP	Hrs	Rate	Total
Sun									1									
									2						St			
Mon									1									
									2						1½			
Tue									1									
									2						2			
Wed									1									
									2						2½			
Thu									1									
									2									
Fri									1									
									2						MP			
Sat									1									
									2						VAC			

Employee Health Insurance Deduction: $ _____   Special Unpaid Leave: From ___ To ___
Employment Ended: ☐ No ☐ Yes Date: _____
Comments/Reason For Late Payroll Submission:

HOL
ADJ

ACCT. #	MEALS ALLOWED	MEALS TAXABLE	PER DIEM ADVANCE	ACCT. #	LODGING ALLOW	LODGING TAXABLE	PER DIEM ADVANCE
ACCT. #	BOX RENTAL	ACCT. #	CAR ALLOW	ACCT. #	MILEAGE ALLOW	MILEAGE TAXABLE	MILEAGE ADVANCE
CHECK ONE: ☐ BOX RENTAL INFORMATION ON FILE ☐ BOX RENTAL INFORMATION ATTACHED				ACCT. #	2ND CAMERA	OTHER	SALARY ADVANCE

CA personnel: We have a Medical Provider Network (MPN) for all work-related injuries and/or illnesses. In the event of an injury, your care will be directed to a physician within the MPN. You may qualify to pre-designate a doctor. For more information, please contact us at 310 440 9675 or wcdept@mediaservices.com.

Total $

BY SIGNING, YOU CERTIFY THAT THE RECORD OF TIME WORKED IS CORRECT. WITHOUT APPROPRIATE DOCUMENTATION, REIMBURSABLE EXPENSES WILL BE CONSIDERED TAXABLE ITEMS.

EMPLOYEE SIGNATURE X _____   APPROVED X _____

Reprint courtesy of Media Services Payroll

with codes for essential time card categories — again, that's car, per diem, box rentals, meals.

Note in the comments section that Joe received a travel day. The rate of that travel day is half his usual rate. So, when calculating the total, make sure those 50 cents (man, Joe really should ask for a raise) are added.

The total is the $1 Joe makes, plus his box rental, per diem, meal stipend, gas reimbursement, and the half-day pay for his travel day. 1.00 + 10.00 + 30.00 + 15.00 + 67.89 + .50 = 124.39

COMPLETED UNION CREW TIME CARD

UNION

Employee Name Jane Doe	Social Security No. 000-00-0000	Week Ending 11/2		
Loan-Out Corporation I.C. Cameras	Federal I.D. No. 00-0000000	**WORK LOCATION REQUIRED** Location City___ County___ Work State___ Foreign ☐		
Production Name Production Accounting: The Movie	Job Classification 1st Ast. Camera / Union No. 111111111	Union Occupation Code and Schedule 111111111		
Production Company Accounting Rocks, LLC	Rate $250/day / Guar. Hrs. 12	Account Code 2205		

Date	Location Zip Code	1st Meal In	Out	2nd Meal In	Out	In	Wrap	Hrs	MP	Acct	St	1½	2	2½	MP		Hrs	Rate	Total
Sun 10/27	99999	7.0	13.0	13.5			19.5	12.0	1 2		40	20	3.5			St	40	$17.8571	714.28
Mon 10/28	99999	7.0	13.0	13.5			19.5	12.0	1 2							1½	20	$26.7857	535.71
Tue 10/29	99999								1 2							2	3.5	$34.7143	121.50
Wed 10/30	99999								1 2							2½			
Thu 10/31	99999	7.0	13.0	13.5			19.5	12.0	1 2										
Fri 11/1	99999	7.0	13.0	13.5			19.5	12.0	1 2							MP			
Sat 11/2	99999	9.0	15.0	15.5	21.5	22.0	25.5	15.5	1 2							VAC			

Employee Health Insurance Deduction: $___	Special Unpaid Leave:			HOL			
Employment Ended: ☐ No ☑ Yes Date: ___	From___ To___			ADJ			
Comments/Reason For Late Payroll Submission: 7 Days Per Diem $30/day. 5 Days Box Rental $20/day.							

ACCT. #	MEALS ALLOWED	MEALS TAXABLE	PER DIEM ADVANCE $210	ACCT. # 3501	LODGING ALLOW	LODGING TAXABLE	PER DIEM ADVANCE
ACCT. # 2299	BOX RENTAL $100	ACCT. #	CAR ALLOW	ACCT. #	MILEAGE ALLOW	MILEAGE TAXABLE	MILEAGE ADVANCE
CHECK ONE:	☑ BOX RENTAL INFORMATION ON FILE ☐ BOX RENTAL INFORMATION ATTACHED			ACCT. #	2ND CAMERA	OTHER	SALARY ADVANCE

CA personnel: We have a Medical Provider Network (MPN) for all work-related injuries and/or illnesses. In the event of an injury, your care will be directed to a physician within the MPN. You may qualify to pre-designate a doctor. For more information, please contact us at 310 440 9675 or wcdept@mediaservices.com.

Total $ $1,681.50

BY SIGNING, YOU CERTIFY THAT THE RECORD OF TIME WORKED IS CORRECT. WITHOUT APPROPRIATE DOCUMENTATION, REIMBURSABLE EXPENSES WILL BE CONSIDERED TAXABLE ITEMS.

EMPLOYEE SIGNATURE X **Jane Doe** _____ APPROVED X _____ **Line Producer/UPM Signature**

Reprint courtesy of Media Services Payroll

BLANK EXHIBIT G

SCREEN ACTORS GUILD PERFORMERS PRODUCTION TIME REPORT – EXHIBIT G

COMPLETED EXHIBIT G (CAST IN AND OUT TIMES)

SCREEN ACTORS GUILD PERFORMERS PRODUCTION TIME REPORT – EXHIBIT G

Return original of this document to the SAG office within two weeks of completion of principal photography

PICTURE TITLE: Production Accounting: The Movie
SHOOTING LOCATION: 12345 Accounting Dr. Accountingland, CA 99955
Please complete in ink. Indicate a.m. or p.m.

PROD. NO. 1111112 DATE 10/21 CONTACT Important Producer PHONE 123-456-7890
IS TODAY A DESIGNATED DAY OFF? Yes ___ No X

Cast	Character	W H S F R T FT**	Report Makeup Wardrobe	Report On Set	Dismiss On Set	Dismiss Makeup Wardrobe	ND Meal	1st Meal Start	1st Meal Finish	2nd Meal Start	2nd Meal Finish	Leave for Location	Arrive on Location	Leave Location	Arrive at Studio	Minors Tutoring Time	No. of Outfits	Performer's Signature
Mike Smith	Numbers McGee	SW	10:00A	10:45A	4:45P	5:00P		2:00P	2:30P			9:00A	9:30A	5:00P	5:30P			M.S.
John Smith	Chet "Money Man" Safe	SW	9:00A	9:45A	4:00P	4:15P		2:00P	2:30P									J.S.

** Work=W Rehearsal=R Start=S Finish=F Hold=H Travel=TR Fitting=FT Test=T

146

BLANK ACTOR TIME CARD

ACTOR'S WEEKLY TIME REPORT

CHECK ONE: SAG ☐ AFTRA ☐

W/E _____   EPISODE # _____

WORK STATUS SYMBOLS KEY

SW START WORK
W   WORK
H   HOLD
R   REHEARSE
WF WORK FINISHED
T   TRAVEL
D   DROP
P   PICK UP

ARTIST'S NAME _____
CORP. NAME _____
PICTURE NAME _____

SOC. SEC. # _____
FED ID # _____
ROLE OF _____

WORK LOCATION REQUIRED

Location ___ City ___ County ___
Work State ___ Foreign ☐
☐ Studio ☐ Local Location ☐ Distant (Overnight) Location

Any finish will be considered an employment end date for purposes of Affordable Care Act compliance.

DAY	DATE	WORK STATUS	TRAVEL LV MTL	ARR LOC	MKUP HAIR	ON SET ST. TIME	FIRST MEAL FROM	TO	SECOND MEAL FROM	TO	DISMISSED SET	ARR MTL	Total Hours	Travel Time Hours	Time Over 8/10 hrs. TT@ 1½	OT@ 1½	OT@ 2X	COMMENTS: NON-DEDUCTIBLE MEALS, STUNT ADJUSTMENTS, ETC.
SUN																		
MON																		
TUE																		
WED																		
THU																		
FRI																		
SAT																		

SPECIAL UNPAID LEAVE:
FROM _____ TO _____

EMPLOYMENT ENDED:
☐ NO ☐ YES DATE: _____

ACCUM WEEKLY HOURS _____
LESS 44/48/24/32 _____
LESS DAILY OT/TT _____
WEEKLY OT HOURS _____

Authorization for payment _____

BASIC HOURLY RATE: _____

CONTRACT TYPE: _____

DAY PLAYER RATE: _____
3 DAY PLAYER RATE: _____
WEEKLY PLAYER RATE: _____

ACTOR ___ SINGER ___ PILOT ___
STUNT ___ LOOPER ___ DANCER ___
SPECIALITY ACT ___ OFF CAM ANN ___
MOW ___ LENGTH ___
THEATRICAL ___
SERIES ½ HR. ___ 1 HR. ___
OTHER (SPECIFY) ___

ACCT CODE	HRS	RATE	TOTALS
DAILY			
WEEKLY			
DAILY OT @ 1½			
DAILY OT @ 2X			
WEEKLY OT			
LOC ALLOW			
STUNT ADJ			
NIGHT PREM			
AGENTS FEE			

ACCT CODE	TOTALS
MEAL PENALTY	
FORCE CALL	
MISC. DED	
REIMB. EXP	
MISC	
OTHER SPECIFY	
TOTAL DUE	
NON PENSION	

COMPLETED ACTOR TIME CARD: DAY PLAYER

ACTOR'S WEEKLY TIME REPORT

WORK STATUS SYMBOLS KEY
- SW START WORK
- W WORK
- H HOLD
- R REHEARSE
- WF WORK FINISHED
- T TRAVEL

WORK LOCATION (City/State/Country) ACCOUNTINGLAND/CA/U.S.

- ARTISTS NAME: JOHN SMITH
- CORP. NAME: N/A
- PICTURE NAME: PRODUCTION ACCOUNTING: THE MOVIE
- SOC. SEC. #: 111-11-1111
- FED ID#: N/A
- ROLE OF: Chet "Money Man" Safe

CHECK ONE
- SAG ✓
- AFTRA ☐
- W/E 10/26
- EPISODE #

DAY	DATE	WORK STATUS	TRAVEL LV MTL	TRAVEL ARR LOC	MK/UP HAIR	ON SET ST. TIME	FIRST MEAL FROM	FIRST MEAL TO	SECOND MEAL FROM	SECOND MEAL TO	DISMISSED SET	DISMISSED APR MTL	Total Hours	Travel Time Hours	Time Over 8/10 hrs. TT@ 1½	OT@ 1½	OT@ 2X	REMARKS NDB, STUNT, ADJ, ETC.
SUN	10/20																	
MON	10/21	SW	9:00A	9:00A	9:00A	9:45A	1:00P	1:30P			4:00P		6.5					
TUE	10/22	H																
WED	10/23	H																
THU	10/24																	
FRI	10/25																	
SAT	10/26	H																

MARITAL STATUS

NO. EXEMPT.

ACCUM WEEKLY HOURS 6.5
LESS 44/48/24/32
LESS DAILY OT/TT
WEEKLY OT HOURS

BASIC, HOURLY RATE:
CONTRACT TYPE:
DAY PLAYER RATE: $1,000
3 DAY PLAYER RATE:
WEEKLY PLAYER RATE:

Authorization for payment

ACCT CODE	HRS		RATE	TOTALS
1401	6.5	DAILY	$1,000	$1,000
		WEEKLY		
		DAILY OT @ 1½		
		DAILY OT @ 2X		
		WEEKLY OT		
		LOC ALLOW		
		STUNT ADJ		
		NIGHT PREM		
		AGENTS FEE		

ACCT CODE	TOTALS
MEAL PENALTY	
FORCE CALL	
MISC. DED	
REIMB. EXP	
MISC	
OTHER SPECIFY	
TOTAL DUE	$1,000.00
NON PENSION	

- MOW
- THEATRICAL X
- SERIES ½ HR. 1 HR.
- OTHER (SPECIFY)
- NO. OF HRS.
- ACTOR X SINGER PILOT
- STUNT LOOPER DANCER
- SPECIALTY ACT OFF CAM ANN

Reprint courtesy of Media Services Payroll

COMPLETED ACTOR TIME CARD: WEEKLY

ACTOR'S WEEKLY TIME REPORT

WORK STATUS SYMBOLS KEY
SW START WORK
W WORK
H HOLD
R REHEARSE
WF WORK FINISHED
T TRAVEL

CHECK ONE: SAG ✓ · AFTRA ☐
W/E 10/26
EPISODE #

WORK LOCATION (City/State/Country) ACCOUNTINGLAND/CA/U.S.
ARTISTS NAME MIKE SMITH
CORP. NAME N/A
PICTURE NAME PRODUCTION ACCOUNTING: THE MOVIE
SOC. SEC. # I'M SICK OF SOCIAL SECURITY NUMBERS
FED ID# N/A
ROLE OF Numbers McGee

DAY	DATE	WORK STATUS	TRAVEL LV MTL	TRAVEL ARR LOC	MKUP HAIR	ON SET ST. TIME	FIRST MEAL FROM	FIRST MEAL TO	SECOND MEAL FROM	SECOND MEAL TO	DISMISSED SET	DISMISSED ARR MTL	Total Hours	Travel Time Hours	T½	OT@ 1½	OT@ 2X	REMARKS NDB, STUNT, ADJ, ETC.
SUN	10/20																	
MON	10/21	SW	9:00A	9:30A	10:00A	10:45A	1:00P	1:30P			5:00P	5:30P	7.0	1.0				
TUE	10/22	W	8:00A	8:30A	9:00A	10:00A	3:00P	3:30P			4:00P	4:30P	7.0	1.0				meal penalty
WED	10/23	W	8:30A	9:00A	9:30A	10:30A	1:00P	1:30P			3:30P	4:00P	6.0	1.0				wardrobe bump
THU	10/24																	
FRI	10/25																	
SAT	10/26	H																

MARITAL STATUS
NO. EXEMPT.

ACCUM WEEKLY HOURS 20.0
LESS 44/48/24/32
LESS DAILY OT/TT
WEEKLY OT HOURS 3.0

BASIC HOURLY RATE:
CONTRACT TYPE:
DAY PLAYER RATE:
3 DAY PLAYER RATE:
WEEKLY PLAYER RATE: $2,190

Authorization for payment

ACCT CODE	HRS	DAILY	RATE	TOTALS
1401	23.0	WEEKLY	$2,190	$2,190
		DAILY OT @ 1½		
		DAILY OT @ 2X		
		WEEKLY OT		
		LOC ALLOW		
		STUNT ADJ		
		NIGHT PREM		
		AGENTS FEE		

ACCT CODE		TOTALS
3540	MEAL PENALTY	$25.00
	FORCE CALL	
	MISC. DED	
	REIMB. EXP.	
2916	MISC	$12.00
	OTHER SPECIFY	
TOTAL DUE		$2,227
NON PENSION		

MOW ___ NO. OF HRS.
THEATRICAL X
SERIES ½ HR. ___ 1 HR.
OTHER (SPECIFY)
ACTOR X · SINGER ___ · PILOT ___
STUNT ___ · LOOPER ___ · DANCER ___
SPECIALTY ACT ___ · OFF CAM ANN ___

Reprint courtesy of Media Services Payroll

Please note: To get all this information, check the actor's start paperwork. Also, when actors are provided transportation, their hours traveled count as hours worked. Mike Smith had a meal penalty one day and brought wardrobe for himself on another day. Those are noted in the bottom right-hand column and added to his pay for the week, similar to Joe and his per diem, box rental, and meal stipend.

All of this info can be found in EP's *The Paymaster* and on the SAG-AFTRA website.

SAMPLE CAST DAY OUT OF DAYS (DOOD)

A **Day Out of Days** is a chart that shows what days each cast member worked and how many total days they worked throughout the production. Day Out of Days forms are not just for cast members. They can include anything from props and picture vehicles to stunts, special equipment, or any additional labor (medics, studio teachers, etc.).

Ideally, the DOOD is locked before the shoot, but sometimes things change (for instance if the weather won't play ball). When that happens, the DOOD is updated and the new version is distributed to all departments.

Let's say you wanted to know how many days the actor playing "Daniel" worked and which specific days he was needed on set. You would see that Daniel's first day (denoted by "SW" [start work]) was Friday, 10/21. He also worked 10/26, 10/27, and 10/28 (his last day, denoted by "WF" [work finished]).

CAST DAY OUT OF DAYS (DOOD)

PRODUCTION ACCOUNTING: THE MOVIE **Yellow Script**
Day Out of Days Report for Cast Members

	Month/Day	10/21	10/22	10/23	10/24	10/25	10/26	10/27	10/28	10/29
	Day of Week	Mon	Tue	Wed	Thu	Fri	Sat	Sun	Mon	Tue
	Shooting Day	1	2	3			4	5	6	7
1.	Numbers McGee	SW	W	W				W		W
2.	Chet "Money Man" Safe	SW								
3.	Penelope			SWF						
4.	Daniel	SW					W	W	WF	
5.	Naoko	SW							W	
6.	John							SW	W	WF
7.	Max		SW					W	W	WF
8.	Alexa								SWF	
9.	Ava						SW			W
10.	Ruthie			SWF						
11.	Andy	SW		W						W
12.	Kim	SW								WF

PRODUCTION ACCOUNTING: THE MOVIE **Yellow Script**
Day Out of Days Report for Cast Members

	Month/Day	10/30	10/31	11/01	11/02	11/03	Co.			
	Day of Week	Wed	Thu	Fri	Sat	Sun	Travel	Work	Hold	Holiday
	Shooting Day	8			9	10				
1.	Numbers McGee	W			W	WF		8		
2.	Chet "Money Man" Safe	W			W	WF		4		
3.	Penelope							1		
4.	Daniel							4		
5.	Naoko	W				WF		4		
6.	John							3		
7.	Max							4		
8.	Alexa							1		
9.	Ava	WF						3		
10.	Ruthie							1		
11.	Andy					WF		4		
12.	Kim							2		

PRODUCTION ACCOUNTING: THE MOVIE **Yellow Script**
Day Out of Days Report for Cast Members

	Month/Day			
	Day of Week	Start	Finish	TOTAL
	Shooting Day			
1.	Numbers McGee	10/21	11/03	8
2.	Chet "Money Man" Safe	10/21	11/03	4
3.	Penelope	10/22	10/22	1
4.	Daniel	10/21	10/28	4
5.	Naoko	10/21	11/03	4
6.	John	10/27	10/29	3
7.	Max	10/22	10/29	4
8.	Alexa	10/28	10/28	1
9.	Ava	10/26	10/30	3
10.	Ruthie	10/23	10/23	1
11.	Andy	10/21	11/03	4
12.	Kim	10/21	10/29	2

The DOOD is generated from Movie Magic Scheduling by the AD.

BLANK DAY PLAYER SAG-AFTRA CONTRACT

SAG·AFTRA. SCREEN ACTORS GUILD
EMPLOYMENT OF DAY PERFORMER FOR LOW BUDGET THEATRICAL FILM

PRODUCTION COMPANY (EMPLOYER)_____DATE_____

DATE EMPLOYMENT STARTS_____ PERFORMER'S NAME _____

ROLE_____ DAILY RATE $ _____

ADDRESS _____

PERFORMER'S TELEPHONE NO._____ WEEKLY* CONVERSION RATE $_____

PRODUCTION TITLE _____

GUARANTEED DATES OF EMPLOYMENT _____

1. Performer has been advised of and does agree ☐ does not agree ☐ to the following terms of the Low Budget Agreement.

    (a) Weekend premiums are waived provided Performer receives required rest period each week.
    (b) Consecutive employment requirement is waived provided scheduling of calls is subject to Performer's availability, except while on overnight locations.

2. Daily overtime through the twelfth hour each day is payable at time-and-one half rates. Overtime on a day involving rehearsal only is payable at straight time rates.

3. If Performer agrees to furnish any wardrobe or wearing apparel for the portrayal of this role, Performer shall receive $_____ per costume per calendar week for such use. (If space is left blank, amount is presumed to be the applicable fee in the Screen Actors Guild Codified Basic Agreement.)

4. All provisions of the collective bargaining agreement between Screen Actors Guild, and Producer, relating to theatrical motion pictures, which are applicable to the employment of the Performer hereunder, shall be deemed incorporated herein except as expressly modified by the current Letter Agreement for Low Budget Theatrical Pictures which is also deemed incorporated herein by reference.

5. (West Coast Performer Only): The Performer (does) (does not) hereby authorize the producer to deduct from the compensation hereinabove specified an amount equal to_____ percent of each installment of compensation due the Performer hereunder, and to pay the amount so deducted to the Motion Picture and Television Relief Fund of America, Inc.

6. Producer makes the material representation that either it is presently a signatory to the SAG collective bargaining agreement covering the employment contracted for herein, or, that the above-referenced photoplay is covered by such collective bargaining agreement under the "Independent Production" provision of the General Provisions of the Screen Actors Guild Codified Basic Agreement.

COMPANY _____ PERFORMER _____

BY _____SOCIAL SECURITY # _____
*NOTE: All weekly rates are 5-day "studio rates".

THE PERFORMER MAY NOT WAIVE ANY PROVISION OF THIS CONTRACT WITHOUT THE PRIOR WRITTEN CONSENT OF SCREEN ACTORS GUILD.

Day Performer Contract Low Budget 6.28   Page 1 of 1

COMPLETED DAY PLAYER SAG-AFTRA CONTRACT

SAG·AFTRA.   **SCREEN ACTORS GUILD**
EMPLOYMENT OF DAY PERFORMER FOR LOW BUDGET THEATRICAL FILM

PRODUCTION COMPANY (EMPLOYER) Accounting Rocks, LLC _____ DATE 10/21 _____

DATE EMPLOYMENT STARTS 10/21 _____ PERFORMER'S NAME John Smith _____

ROLE Chet "Money Man" Safe _____ DAILY RATE $ 1,000 _____

ADDRESS ___ 54321 Fake Street, Somewhereville, CA 99999-9999 _____

PERFORMER'S TELEPHONE NO. 111-222-3333 _____ WEEKLY* CONVERSION RATE $ n/a _____

PRODUCTION TITLE Production Accounting: The Movie _____

GUARANTEED DATES OF EMPLOYMENT 10/21, 10/31, 11/02, 11/03 _____

1. Performer has been advised of and does agree ☑ does not agree ☐ to the following terms of the Low Budget Agreement.

    (a) Weekend premiums are waived provided Performer receives required rest period each week.
    (b) Consecutive employment requirement is waived provided scheduling of calls is subject to Performer's availability, except while on overnight locations.

2. Daily overtime through the twelfth hour each day is payable at time-and-one half rates. Overtime on a day involving rehearsal only is payable at straight time rates.

3. If Performer agrees to furnish any wardrobe or wearing apparel for the portrayal of this role, Performer shall receive $ _n/a_ per costume per calendar week for such use. (If space is left blank, amount is presumed to be the applicable fee in the Screen Actors Guild Codified Basic Agreement.)

4. All provisions of the collective bargaining agreement between Screen Actors Guild, and Producer, relating to theatrical motion pictures, which are applicable to the employment of the Performer hereunder, shall be deemed incorporated herein except as expressly modified by the current Letter Agreement for Low Budget Theatrical Pictures which is also deemed incorporated herein by reference.

5. (West Coast Performer Only): The Performer (does) (does not) hereby authorize the producer to deduct from the compensation hereinabove specified an amount equal to _n/a_ percent of each installment of compensation due the Performer hereunder, and to pay the amount so deducted to the Motion Picture and Television Relief Fund of America, Inc.

6. Producer makes the material representation that either it is presently a signatory to the SAG collective bargaining agreement covering the employment contracted for herein, or, that the above-referenced photoplay is covered by such collective bargaining agreement under the "Independent Production" provision of the General Provisions of the Screen Actors Guild Codified Basic Agreement.

COMPANY Accounting Rocks, LLC _____ PERFORMER John Smith's signature _____

BY Producer's Signature _____ SOCIAL SECURITY # 111-11-1111 _____
*NOTE: All weekly rates are 5-day "studio rates".

THE PERFORMER MAY NOT WAIVE ANY PROVISION OF THIS CONTRACT WITHOUT THE PRIOR WRITTEN CONSENT OF SCREEN ACTORS GUILD.

Day Performer Contract Low Budget 6.28   Page 1 of 1

BLANK WEEKLY SAG-AFTRA CONTRACT

SAG·AFTRA. SCREEN ACTORS GUILD-AMERICAN FEDERATION OF TELEVISION AND RADIO ARTISTS EMPLOYMENT OF WEEKLY PERFORMER FOR LOW BUDGET THEATRICAL MOTION PICTURES

THIS AGREEMENT, made this _____ day of _____, 20 ___, between

_____, hereinafter called "Producer",

and _____, hereinafter called "Performer".

WITNESSETH:

1. PHOTOPLAY, ROLE, SALARY, AND GUARANTEE. Producer hereby engages Performer to render services in the role of_____ in a photoplay, the working title of which is now_____, at the salary of $_____ per week. Performer accepts such engagement upon the terms herein specified. Producer guarantees that it will furnish Performer not less than _____ weeks employment. (If this blank is not filled in, the guarantee shall be one week).

2. TERM. The term of employment hereunder shall begin on_____/on or about *_____.

3. PERFORMER has been advised of and does agree[_____]/does not agree[_____] to the following terms of the SAG-AFTRA Low Budget Agreement for Theatrical Motion Pictures:

    (a) Weekend premiums are waived provided Performer receives required rest period each week.

    (b) Consecutive employment requirement is waived provided scheduling of calls is subject to Performer's availability, except while on overnight locations. With the exception of a partial final work week, Performer will be paid in units of no less than one full week.

4. DAILY OVERTIME through the 12th hour shall be paid at time and one-half. Daily overtime beginning with the 13th work hour shall be paid at double time rates.

5. BASIC CONTRACT. All provisions of the current SAG-AFTRA Agreement for Independent Producers of Theatrical Motion Pictures, which are applicable to the employment of the Performer hereunder, shall be deemed incorporated herein except as expressly modified by the current SAG-AFTRA Agreement for Low Budget Theatrical Motion Pictures which is also deemed incorporated herein by reference.

6. PERFORMER'S ADDRESS. All notices which the Producer is required or may desire to give the Performer may be given either by mailing the same addressed to the Performer at: _____ or such notice may be given to the Performer personally, either orally or in writing.

7. PERFORMER'S TELEPHONE. The Performer must keep the Producer's casting office or the assistant director of said photoplay advised as to where the Performer may be reached by telephone without unreasonable delay. The current telephone number of the Performer is _____

BLANK WEEKLY SAG-AFTRA CONTRACT Page 2

8. MOTION PICTURES AND TELEVISION RELIEF FUND (For West Coast Performers Only). The Performer ☐(does) ☐(does not) hereby authorize the Producer to deduct from the compensation hereinabove specified an amount equal to _____ percent of each installment of compensation due the Performer hereunder, and to pay the amount so deducted to the Motion Picture and Television Relief Fund of America, Inc.

9. FURNISHING OF WARDROBE. The ☐(Producer) ☐(Performer) agrees to furnish all modern wardrobe and wearing apparel reasonably necessary for the portrayal of said role. If Performer agrees to furnish any wardrobe or wearing apparel for the portrayal of this role, Performer shall receive $_____per costume per calendar week for such use. (If is left blank, amount is presumed to be t he applicable fee in the current SAG-AFTRA Agreement for Independent Producers of Theatrical Motion Pictures).

10. ARBITRATION OF DISPUTES. S hould any dispute or controversy arise between the parties hereto with reference to this contract, or employment herein provided for, such dispute or controversy shall be settled and determined by conciliation and arbitration in accordance with the conciliation and arbitration provisions of the collective bargaining agreement between the Producer and SAG-AFTRA relating to theatrical motion pictures, and such provisions are hereby referred to and by such reference incorporated herein and made a part of this agreement with the same effect as though the same were set forth herein in detail.

11. Producer makes the material representation that it is presently a signatory to the SAG-AFTRA Agreement for Low Budget Theatrical Motion Pictures covering the employment contracted for herein.

IN WITNESS WHEREOF, the parties have executed this agreement in the day and year first above written.

PRODUCER_____ PERFORMER_____

BY_____ SOCIAL SECURITY #_____

*The "on or about" clause may only be used when the contract is delivered to the Performer at least seven days before the starting date, otherwise a specific starting date must be provided.

THE PERFORMER MAY NOT WAIVE ANY PROVISION OF THIS CONTRACT WITHOUT THE PRIOR WRITTEN CONSENT OF SAG-AFTRA.

COMPLETED WEEKLY SAG-AFTRA CONTRACT

SCREEN ACTORS GUILD-AMERICAN FEDERATION OF TELEVISION AND RADIO ARTISTS EMPLOYMENT OF WEEKLY PERFORMER FOR LOW BUDGET THEATRICAL MOTION PICTURES

THIS AGREEMENT, made this __21__ day of __October__, 201_9_, between

Accounting Rocks, LLC _____, hereinafter called "Producer",

and Mike Smith _____, hereinafter called "Performer".

WITNESSETH:

1. PHOTOPLAY, ROLE, SALARY, AND GUARANTEE. P roducer hereby engages Performer to render services in the role of Numbers McGee_____ in a photoplay, the working title of which is now _Production Accounting: The Movie_, at the salary of $ 2,190_____ per week. Performer accepts such engagement upon the terms herein specified. Producer guarantees that it will furnish Performer not less than ___3_____ weeks employment. (If this blank is not filled in, the guarantee shall be one week).

2. TERM. The term of employment hereunder shall begin on_____/on or about 1̶0/21_____.

3. PERFORMER has been advised of and do es agree [✓] does not agree [   ] to the following terms of the SAG-AFTRA Low Budget Agreement for Theatrical Motion Pictures:

    (a) Weekend premiums are waived provided Performer receives required rest period each week.

    (b) Consecutive employment requirement is waived provided scheduling of calls is subject to Performer's availability, except while on overnight locations. With the exception of a partial final work week, Performer will be paid in units of no less than one full week.

4. DAILY OVERTIME through the 12th hour shall be paid at time and one-half. Daily overtime beginning with the 13th work hour shall be paid at double time rates.

5. BASIC CONTRACT. All provisions of the current SAG-AFTRA Agreement for Independent Producers of Theatrical Motion Pictures, which are applicable to the employment of the Performer hereunder, shall be deemed incorporated herein except as expressly modified by the current SAG-AFTRA Agreement for Low Budget Theatrical Motion Pictures which is also deemed incorporated herein by reference.

6. PERFORMER'S ADDRESS. All notices which the Producer is required or may desire to give the Performer may be given either by mailing the same addressed to the Performer at: A Hidden Castle Guarded by a Dragon_____ or such notice may be given to the Performer personally, either orally or in writing.

7. PERFORMER'S TELEPHONE. The Performer must keep the Producer's casting office or the assistant director of said photoplay advised as to where the Performer may be r eached by telephone without unreasonable delay. The current telephone number of the Performer is _999-999-9999____

THE CLERK

COMPLETED WEEKLY SAG-AFTRA CONTRACT Page 2

8. MOTION PICTURES AND TELEVISION RELIEF FUND (For West Coast Performers Only). The Performer ☐ (does) ☑ (does not) hereby authorize the Producer to deduct from the compensation hereinabove specified an amount equal to _____ percent of each installment of compensation due the Performer hereunder, and to pay the amount so deducted to the Motion Picture and Television Relief Fund of America, Inc.

9. FURNISHING OF WARDROBE. The ☑ (Producer) ☐ (Performer) agrees to furnish all modern wardrobe and wearing apparel reasonably necessary for the portrayal of said role. If Performer agrees to furnish any wardrobe or wearing apparel for the portrayal of this role, Performer shall receive $____ per costume per calendar week for such use. (If is left blank, amount is presumed to be the applicable fee in the current SAG-AFTRA Agreement for Independent Producers of Theatrical Motion Pictures).

10. ARBITRATION OF DISPUTES. Should any dispute or controversy arise between the parties hereto with reference to this contract, or employment herein provided for, such dispute or controversy shall be settled and determined by conciliation and arbitration in accordance with the conciliation and arbitration provisions of the collective bargaining agreement between the Producer and SAG-AFTRA relating to theatrical motion pictures, and such provisions are hereby referred to and by such reference incorporated herein and made a part of this agreement with the same effect as though the same were set forth herein in detail.

11. Producer makes the material representation that it is presently a signatory to the SAG-AFTRA Agreement for Low Budget Theatrical Motion Pictures covering the employment contracted for herein.

IN WITNESS WHEREOF, the parties have executed this agreement in the day and year first above written.

PRODUCER Accounting Rocks, LLC   PERFORMER Mike Smith's Signature

BY Producer's Signature   SOCIAL SECURITY # 111-11-1111

*The "on or about" clause may only be used when the contract is delivered to the Performer at least seven days before the starting date, otherwise a specific starting date must be provided.

THE PERFORMER MAY NOT WAIVE ANY PROVISION OF THIS CONTRACT WITHOUT THE PRIOR WRITTEN CONSENT OF SAG-AFTRA.

WHAT A BUDGET LOOKS LIKE (BASED ON A GAME SHOW)

ACCOUNTING ROCKS - SEASON #1 - SD
Accounting Productions

Executive Producer(s): TBD
Line Producer: TBD
Prepared By: TBD
Date Prepared/Modified:
Budget Revision #: V1
# of Episodes: 35
Per Episode Cost: $1.00

Start Date: TBD
Finish Date: TBD
Total Weeks: 16
Shoot Weeks (Field/Studio): 3
Post Weeks: 7
Wrap Weeks: 1

Acct#	Category Description	Page	Total
6000	Script/Researchers	1	$8,974
6100	Cast	1	$164,776
6150	Producers	2	$72,460
6175	Directors	2	$20,819
	Total Above-The-Line		**$267,028**
6190	Production Staff	4	$123,843
6200	Music	5	$14,502
6250	Insurance	5	$21,500
6275	General Expenses	6	$62,300
6350	Set Design/Construction/Dressing	6	$52,308
6375	Lighting	7	$87,669
6450	Make-Up/Hair/Wardrobe	8	$18,080
6475	Crew	9	$55,637
6500	Facilities/Equipment	11	$69,243
	Total Production		**$505,082**
7100	Post Production	13	$97,880
	Total Post Production		**$97,880**
9100	Production Fee (0 excluded)		$25,000
9200	Legal Fee		$11,000
	Grand Total		**$905,990**

ACCOUNTING ROCKS

Acct#	Description	Amt	Units	X	Rate	Sub T	Total
6000	**Script/Researchers**						
6001	Script Consultant (Exempt)						
	Consultant TBD #1 (3 weeks prep)	3	Weeks	1	500	1,500	
	Consultant TBD #1 (3 weeks shoot)	3	Weeks	1	500	1,500	
	Consultant TBD #2 (Host) (shoot weeks only)	3	Weeks	1	500	1,500	
	Script Coordinator (3 weeks prep)	3	Weeks	1	500	1,500	
	Script Coordinator (3 weeks shoot)	3	Weeks	1	500	1,500	
	Total						$7,500
	Total Fringes						
	FICA	6.2%			7,500	465	
	FICA MED	1.45%			7,500	109	
	FUTA	0.8%			7,500	60	
	SUTA	6.2%			7,500	465	
	BENEFITS	5%			7,500	375	$1,474
Account Total for 6000							**$8,974**
6100	**Cast**						
6101	OAT- Host/Star (Exempt)						
	Host TBD	35	Epis...	1	500	17,500	
	Total						$17,500
6102	OAT - Principal Player (Exempt)						
	Contestants	35	Epis...	4	300	42,000	
	On call Contestants on tape days	15	Days	4	50	3,000	
	Rehearsal Days	2	Days	4	50	400	
	Total						$45,400
6103	Reality Casting Director (Exempt)						
	Casting Director Prep	6	Weeks	1	700	4,200	
	Casting Director shoot	3	Weeks	1	700	2,100	
	Associate Casting Director prep	6	Weeks	1	700	4,200	
	Associate Casting Director shoot	3	Weeks	1	700	2,100	
	Total						$12,600
6104	Cash Prizes						
	Gift Certificates	35	Epis...	1	75	2,625	
	Total						$2,625
6105	Contestant Background checks						
	Background checks on contestants	250	Allow	1	300	75,000	
	Total						$75,000

ACCOUNTING ROCKS

Continuation of Account 6177

Acct#	Description	Amt	Units	X	Rate	Sub T	Total
	Total						$3,600
6180	Stage Manager (Non-Exempt)						
	TBD	18	Days	1	150	2,700	
	TBD - OT	18	Days	1	50	900	
	Total						$3,600
6181	Script Supervisor (Exempt)						
	TBD	6	Weeks	1	500	3,000	
	Total						$3,000
	Total Fringes						
	FICA	6.2%			17,400	1,079	
	FICA MED	1.45%			17,400	252	
	FUTA	0.8%			17,400	139	
	SUTA	6.2%			17,400	1,079	
	BENEFITS	5%			17,400	870	$3,419
Account Total for 6175							**$20,819**
	Total Above-The-Line						**$267,028**

160

THE CLERK

ACCOUNTING ROCKS

Acct#	Description	Amt	Units	X	Rate	Sub T	Total
	Total Fringes						
	FICA	6.2%			75,500	4,681	
	FICA MED	1.45%			75,500	1,095	
	FUTA	0.8%			30,000	240	
	SUTA	6.2%			30,000	1,860	
	BENEFITS	5%			75,500	3,775	$11,651
Account Total for 6100							**$164,776**
6150 Producers							
6151	Executive Producer (Exempt)						
	TBD	14	Weeks	1	1,000	14,000	
	Total						$14,000
6153	Supervising Producer (Exempt)						
	TBD #1	14	Weeks	1	800	11,200	
	TBD#2	14	Weeks	1	800	11,200	
	Total						$22,400
6154	Exec In Charge Of Production (Exempt)						
	TBD	16	Weeks	1	800	12,800	
	Total						$12,800
6156	Show Producer (Exempt)						
	TBD #1	9	Weeks	1	700	6,300	
	TBD #2	9	Weeks	1	700	6,300	
	Total						$12,600
	Total Fringes						
	FICA	6.2%			61,800	3,832	
	FICA MED	1.45%			61,800	896	
	FUTA	0.8%			40,600	325	
	SUTA	6.2%			40,600	2,517	
	BENEFITS	5%			61,800	3,090	$10,660
Account Total for 6150							**$72,460**
6175 Directors							
6176	Director (Non-Exempt)						
	TBD	18	Days	1	200	3,600	
	TBD - OT	18	Days	1	200	3,600	
	Total						$7,200
6177	Associate Director (Non-Exempt)						
	TBD	18	Days	1	100	1,800	
	TBD - OT	18	Days	1	100	1,800	

ACCOUNTING ROCKS

Acct#	Description	Amt	Units	X	Rate	Sub T	Total
6190 Production Staff							
6191	Associate Producer (Non-Exempt)						
	TBD #1 (prep, tape/edit, edit only)	9	Weeks	1	500	4,500	
	TBD #1 - OT Tape Days	18	Days	1	25	450	
	Subtotal					$4,950	
	TBD #2 (prep,tape/edit, edit only)	9	Weeks	1	500	4,500	
	TBD #2 - OT Tape Days	18	Days	1	25	450	
	Subtotal					$4,950	
	TBD #3 (prep, tape/edit, edit only)	9	Weeks	1	500	4,500	
	TBD #3 - OT Tape Days	18	Days	1	25	450	
	Subtotal					$4,950	
	Total						$14,850
6192	Talent Coordinator (Exempt)						
	Coordinator #1 (prep, shoot/tape)	9	Weeks	1	500	4,500	
	Coordinator #2 (prep, shoot/tape)	9	Weeks	1	500	4,500	
	Total						$9,000
6194	Post Production Supervisor (Exempt)						
	TBD (prep, edit, wrap)	10	Weeks	1	600	6,000	
	Total						$6,000
6196	Production Coordinator (Non-Exempt)						
	TBD (prep, edit, wrap)	9	Weeks	1	600	5,400	
	Total						$5,400
6197	Production Accountant (Non-Exempt)						
	TBD Prep,tape/edit, edit only, wrap	16	Weeks	1	700	11,200	
	Total						$11,200
6198	Production Assistant (Non-Exempt)						
	Recruiter #1 Prep,shoot	7	Weeks	1	500	3,500	
	Recruiter #2 Prep, Shoot	7	Weeks	1	500	3,500	
	Recruiter #3 Prep, Shoot	7	Weeks	1	500	3,500	
	Recruiter #4 Prep, Shoot	7	Weeks	1	500	3,500	
	Subtotal					$14,000	
	Script PA Prep, Shoot	6	Weeks	1	500	3,000	
	Script PA - OT Tape Days	18	Days	1	25	450	
	Subtotal					$3,450	
	Office PA Prep,tape/edit, edit only, wrap	14	Weeks	1	500	7,000	
	Subtotal					$7,000	
	Set PA #1 Prep, shoot, wrap	5	Weeks	1	500	2,500	
	Set PA #1 - OT Tape Days	18	Days	1	25	450	
	Subtotal					$2,950	

THE CLERK

ACCOUNTING ROCKS

Continuation of Account 6198

Acct#	Description	Amt	Units	X	Rate	Sub T	Total
	Set PA #2 Prep, shoot, wrap	5	Weeks	1	500	2,500	
	Set PA #2 - OT Tape Days	18	Days	1	25	450	
	Subtotal					$2,950	
	PA #3 Prep, tape/edit, edit	10	Weeks	1	500	5,000	
	PA #3 - OT Tape Days	18	Days	1	25	450	
	Subtotal					$5,450	
	Post PA #4 Prep, edit, wrap	10	Weeks	1	500	5,000	
	Total						$40,800
6199	Post Producer (Exempt)						
	TBD #1 Prep, edit, wrap	13	Weeks	1	500	6,500	
	TBD #2 Prep, edit, wrap	10	Weeks	1	500	5,000	
	TBD #3 Prep, edit, wrap	10	Weeks	1	500	5,000	
	Total						$16,500
	Total Fringes						
	FICA	6.2%			103,750	6,432	
	FICA MED	1.45%			103,750	1,504	
	FUTA	0.8%			99,550	796	
	SUTA	6.2%			99,550	6,172	
	BENEFITS	5%			103,750	5,188	$20,093
Account Total for 6190							**$123,843**
6200	**Music**						
6206	Music Rights						
		1		1	5,000	5,000	
	Total						$5,000
6207	Other Charges						
	Music Supervisor	10	Weeks	1	800	8,000	
	Total						$8,000
	Total Fringes						
	FICA	6.2%			8,000	496	
	FICA MED	1.45%			8,000	116	
	FUTA	0.8%			7,000	56	
	SUTA	6.2%			7,000	434	
	BENEFITS	5%			8,000	400	$1,502
Account Total for 6200							**$14,502**
6250	**Insurance**						
6251	Production Package						
		1	Allow	1	10,000	10,000	

ACCOUNTING ROCKS

Continuation of Account 6251

Acct#	Description	Amt	Units	X	Rate	Sub T	Total
	Total						$10,000
6252	General Liability/ Umbrella Insurance						
		1	Allow	1	6,000	6,000	
	Total						$6,000
6255	Auto Liability Insurance						
		1	Allow	1	500	500	
	Total						$500
6258	Insurance-Other Charges						
	E & O	1	Allow	1	5,000	5,000	
	Total						$5,000
Account Total for 6250							**$21,500**
6275	**General Expenses**						
6278	Office Supplies						
		1	Allow	1	3,000	3,000	
	Total						$3,000
6280	Office Rent						
	Offices	3	Mon...	6	1,000	18,000	
	Shared	3	Mon...	8	500	12,000	
	Cubes	3	Mon...	20	400	24,000	
	Total						$54,000
6281	Postage/Fed Ex						
		1	Allow	1	1,500	1,500	
	Total						$1,500
6285	Local Parking/Mileage and Gas						
	Set Mileage	4	Mon...	1	200	800	
	Total						$800
6286	General-Other Charges						
	Misc Studio Charges	1	Allow	1	3,000	3,000	
	Total						$3,000
Account Total for 6275							**$62,300**
6350	**Set Design/Construction/Dressing**						
3651	Set Designer/Art Director (Exempt)						
	TBD	5	Weeks	1	1,000	5,000	
	Total						$5,000
6352	Set Decorator (Exempt)						
	On Set Dresser TBD	5	Weeks	1	1,000	5,000	
	Set Dresser TBD	10	Days	1	200	2,000	
	Total						$7,000

ACCOUNTING ROCKS

Acct#	Description	Amt	Units	X	Rate	Sub T	Total
6354	Materials/Models/Blueprints						
	walls reveal set	1	Allow	1	100	100	
	walls bar set	1	Allow	1	5,000	5,000	
	walls couch set	1	Allow	1	15,000	15,000	
	Total						$20,100
6357	Set Rentals						
	Signs	5	Weeks	1	250	1,250	
	Total						$1,250
6359	Set Dressing Purchase						
	furn & props-reveal set	1	Allow	1	3,000	3,000	
	furn & props-bar set	1	Allow	1	5,000	5,000	
	furn & props-couch set	1	Allow	1	4,000	4,000	
	Total						$12,000
6361	Storage						
		12	Mon...	1	300	3,600	
	Total						$3,600
6362	Set-Other Charges						
	strike & trucking	1	Allow	1	1,000	1,000	
	Total						$1,000
	Total Fringes						
	FICA	6.2%			12,000	744	
	FICA MED	1.45%			12,000	174	
	FUTA	0.8%			12,000	96	
	SUTA	6.2%			12,000	744	
	BENEFITS	5%			12,000	600	$2,358
Account Total for 6350							**$52,308**
6375	**Lighting**						
6376	Lighting Designer (Non-Exempt)						
	Lighting Director	21	Days	1	200	4,200	
	Lighting Director - OT	18	Days	1	150	2,700	
	Total						$6,900
6377	Gaffer (Non-Exempt)						
	TBD	21	Days	1	200	4,200	
	TBD - OT	18	Days	1	135	2,430	
	Total						$6,630
6378	Lightboard Operator/Elec (Non-Exempt)						
	TBD	21	Days	1	200	4,200	
	TBD - OT	18	Days	1	127.5	2,295	
	Total						$6,495

ACCOUNTING ROCKS

Acct#	Description	Amt	Units	X	Rate	Sub T	Total
6380	Electrician (Non-Exempt)						
	TBD #1	21	Days	1	200	4,200	
	TBD #1 - OT	18	Days	1	200	3,600	
	Subtotal					$7,800	
	TBD #2	10	Days	1	200	2,000	
	TBD #2 - OT	10	Days	1	200	2,000	
	Subtotal					$4,000	
	TBD #3	5	Days	1	200	1,000	
	TBD #3 - OT	5	Days	1	200	1,000	
	Subtotal					$2,000	
	Total						$13,800
6381	Lighting Rentals						
	VL2500 Spot 12	5	Weeks	1	2,000	10,000	
	VL2500 Wash 6	5	Weeks	1	1,220	6,100	
	Source 4 Leko Body 36	5	Weeks	1	400	2,000	
	Source 4 Leko Lens 36	5	Weeks	1	200	1,000	
	Source 4 Par Body 18	5	Weeks	1	300	1,500	
	Road Hog Full Boar 1	5	Weeks	1	475	2,375	
	CC20 Sensor Hot Dimmer Module 12	5	Weeks	1	150	750	
	SPG Stinger 10 Foot 20	5	Weeks	1	56	280	
	SPG Stinger 20 Foot 20	5	Weeks	1	70	350	
	SPG 2Fer 20	5	Weeks	1	84	420	
	Subtotal					$24,775	
	Tax for Rental	10	%	1	24,775	$2,478	
	Total						$27,253
6383	Lighting Contingency						
	Misc	1	Allow	1	20,000	20,000	
	Total						$20,000
	Total Fringes						
	FICA	6.2%			33,825	2,097	
	FICA MED	1.45%			33,825	490	
	FUTA	0.8%			33,025	264	
	SUTA	6.2%			33,025	2,048	
	BENEFITS	5%			33,825	1,691	$6,591
Account Total for 6375							**$87,669**
6450	**Make-Up/Hair/Wardrobe**						
6451	Make-Up Stylist (Non-Exempt)						
	TBD	17	Days	1	125	2,125	
	TBD - OT	17	Days	1	25	425	
	Total						$2,550
6452	Make-Up Assistant (Non-Exempt)						

ACCOUNTING ROCKS

Continuation of Account 6452

Acct#	Description	Amt	Units	X	Rate	Sub T	Total
	TBD	17	Days	1	125	2,125	
	TBD - OT	17	Days	1	25	425	
	Total						$2,550
6455	Wardrobe Stylist/Merchandiser (Non-Exempt)						
	TBD	17	Days	1	125	2,125	
	TBD - OT	17	Days	1	125	2,125	
	Total						$4,250
6456	Wardrobe/Merchandising Asst (Non-Exempt)						
	TBD	20	Days	1	100	2,000	
	Total						$2,000
6457	Wardrobe Purchases						
	Host	1	Allow	1	4,000	4,000	
	Total						$4,000
6459	Wardrobe Cleaning						
		1	Allow	1	500	500	
	Total						$500
	Total Fringes						
	FICA	6.2%			11,350	704	
	FICA MED	1.45%			11,350	165	
	FUTA	0.8%			11,350	91	
	SUTA	6.2%			11,350	704	
	BENEFITS	5%			11,350	568	$2,230
Account Total for 6450							**$18,080**
6475 Crew							
6477	Technical Director (Non-Exempt)						
	Technical Director	21	Days	1	125	2,625	
	Technical Director - OT	18	Days	1	25	450	
	Subtotal						$3,075
	Tech Manager	21	Days	1	125	2,625	
	Tech Manager - OT	18	Days	1	25	450	
	Total						$6,150
6478	Camera Operator - Studio (Non-Exempt)						
	TBD #1	18	Days	1	125	2,250	
	TBD #1 - OT	18	Days	1	25	450	
	Subtotal						$2,700
	TBD #2	18	Days	1	125	2,250	
	TBD #2 - OT	18	Days	1	25	450	
	Subtotal						$2,700
	TBD #3	18	Days	1	125	2,250	

ACCOUNTING ROCKS

Continuation of Account 6478

Acct#	Description	Amt	Units	X	Rate	Sub T	Total
	TBD #3 - OT	18	Days	1	25	450	
	Subtotal					$2,700	
	TBD #4	18	Days	1	125	2,250	
	TBD #4 - OT	18	Days	1	25	450	
	Subtotal					$2,700	
	Total						$10,800
6479	Video Operator (Non-Exempt)						
	Video Control	18	Days	1	125	2,250	
	Video Control - OT	18	Days	1	25	450	
	Total						$2,700
6480	Video Tape Operator (Non-Exempt)						
	TBD	18	Days	1	125	2,250	
	TBD - OT	18	Days	1	25	450	
	Total						$2,700
6483	Audio Mixer/A1 (Non-Exempt)						
	TBD #1	18	Days	1	125	2,250	
	TBD #1 - OT	18	Days	1	25	450	
	Subtotal					$2,700	
	TBD #2	18	Days	1	125	2,250	
	TBD #2 - OT	18	Days	1	25	450	
	Subtotal					$2,700	
	Total						$5,400
6484	Audio Utility (Non-Exempt)						
	TBD #1 (head)	18	Days	1	125	2,250	
	TBD #1 (head) - OT	18	Days	1	25	450	
	Subtotal					$2,700	
	TBD #2	18	Days	1	125	2,250	
	TBD #2 - OT	18	Days	1	25	450	
	Subtotal					$2,700	
	Total						$5,400
6485	Camera Utility (Non-Exempt)						
	TBD #1 (Head)	18	Days	1	125	2,250	
	TBD #1 (Head) - OT	18	Days	1	25	450	
	Subtotal					$2,700	
	TBD #2	18	Days	1	125	2,250	
	TBD #2 - OT	18	Days	1	25	450	
	Subtotal					$2,700	
	TBD #3	18	Days	1	125	2,250	
	TBD #3 - OT	18	Days	1	25	450	
	Subtotal					$2,700	
	Total						$8,100

ACCOUNTING ROCKS

Acct#	Description	Amt	Units	X	Rate	Sub T	Total
6488	Teleprompter Operator (Non-Exempt)						
	TBD	17	Days	1	125	2,125	
	TBD - OT	17	Days	1	25	425	
	Total						$2,550
6489	Jib Op - Studio (Non-Exempt)						
	TBD	18	Days	1	125	2,250	
	TBD - OT	18	Days	1	25	450	
	Total						$2,700
	Total Fringes						
	FICA	6.2%			46,500	2,883	
	FICA MED	1.45%			46,500	674	
	FUTA	0.8%			46,500	372	
	SUTA	6.2%			46,500	2,883	
	BENEFITS	5%			46,500	2,325	$9,137
Account Total for 6475							**$55,637**
6500	**Facilities/Equipment**						
6501	Equipment Rental - Misc						
		1	Allow	1	4,000	4,000	
	Total						$4,000
6502	Equipment Rental - Sound						
	Audio Sweetening	35	Epis...	1	700	24,500	
	Total						$24,500
6504	Dollys/Jibs						
	Rental	5	Weeks	1	700	3,500	
	Total						$3,500
6505	Record Stock/Tape Stock						
	Masters (2/show - digi)	80	Tapes	1	10	800	
	Audition Tapes (64 min DV Cam)	200	Tapes	1	10	2,000	
	Tape day tapes (7/episode - digi)	35	Epis...	7	12	2,940	
	Rehearsal tapes (digi)	20	Tapes	1	12	240	
	DVDs (Execs)	2	epis...	7	0.25	4	
	DVDs	6	epis...	6	0.25	9	
	Total						$5,993
6511	Craft Services Fees (Non-Payroll - 100%)						
	Staff/Crew Lunches	15	Days	1	300	4,500	
	Total						$4,500
6522	Equipment Purchase - Sound						
	Batteries for Mics & PL	5	Weeks	1	100	500	
	Total						$500
6523	Equipment Purchase - Camera						

ACCOUNTING ROCKS

Continuation of Account 6523

Acct#	Description	Amt	Units	X	Rate	Sub T	Total
	DV Cam (casting)	1	Allow	1	1,500	1,500	
	Total						$1,500
6524	Flypack						
	All equipment included except lighting	5	Weeks	1	1,800	9,000	
	1 wk load in						
	3 wks of taping						
	1 wk of striking						
	Total						$9,000
6525	Studio Rental						
	Studio Walls (includes power, AC, parking, dressin...	21	Days	1	750	15,750	
	Total						$15,750
Account Total for 6500							**$69,243**
	Total Production						**$505,082**

ACCOUNTING ROCKS

Acct#	Description	Amt	Units	X	Rate	Sub T	Total
7100 Post Production							
7101	Edit System Rental						
	Avid Rental #1	2	Weeks	1	700	1,400	
	Avid Rental #2	1	Week	2	700	1,400	
	Avid Rental #3	1	Week	4	700	2,800	
	Avid Rental #4	1	Week	6	700	4,200	
	Avid Rental #5	2	Weeks	7	700	9,800	
	Digi Beta Deck Rental #1	2	Weeks	8	100	1,600	
	Digi Beta Deck Rental #2	1	Week	12	100	1,200	
	Unity Rental	13	Weeks	1	1,000	13,000	
	Avid Rental #1 (w/ deck)	13	Weeks	1	700	9,100	
	Avid Rental #2 (w/ deck)	13	Weeks	1	700	9,100	
	Room Rental	1	Mon...	10	500	5,000	
	Total						$58,600
7103	Editor (Non-Exempt)						
	TBD #1 (35 Sessions)	35	Sess...	1	125	4,375	
	TBD #2 (35 Sessions)	35	Sess...	1	125	4,375	
	TBD #3 (35 Sessions)	35	Sess...	1	125	4,375	
	TBD #4 (35 Sessions)	35	Sess...	1	125	4,375	
	TBD #5 (35 Sessions)	35	Sess...	1	125	4,375	
	TBD #6 (35 Sessions)	35	Sess...	1	125	4,375	
	Total						$26,250
7104	Assistant Editor (Non-Exempt)						
	TBD #1	12	Weeks	1	100	1,200	
	TBD #2	12	Weeks	1	100	1,200	
	Total						$2,400
7106	Dubs						
		1	Allow	1	5,000	5,000	
	Total						$5,000
	Total Fringes						
	FICA	6.2%			28,650	1,776	
	FICA MED	1.45%			28,650	415	
	FUTA	0.8%			28,650	229	
	SUTA	6.2%			28,650	1,776	
	BENEFITS	5%			28,650	1,432	$5,630
Account Total for 7100							**$97,880**
	Total Post Production						**$97,880**

ACCOUNTING ROCKS

Acct#	Description	Amt	Units	X	Rate	Sub T	Total
	Production Fee (0 excluded)						$25,000
	Legal Fee						$11,000
	Grand Total						**$905,990**

ACCOUNTING ROCKS

Fringe Breakdown Summary

Fringe	Description	% or Rate	Unit	Cutoff	Total
Payroll Taxes & Fringe	All Taxes and Benefits	17%		0	$0
AFTRA PH&W	AFTRA Pension, Health, & Welfare	15.1%		0	$0
FICA	Social Security Taxes	6.2%		106,800	$25,189
FICA MED	Medicare Taxes	1.45%		0	$5,891
FUTA	Federal Unemployement Taxes	0.8%		7,000	$2,669
SUTA	State Unemployement Taxes	6.2%		7,000	$20,682
BENEFITS	Benefit Costs	5%		0	$20,314
W/C	Workers Compensation Insurance	4%		0	$0
ALL FRINGES					**$74,744**

For independent projects, budgets are usually built by the producer of either the company or the show, but most studios like the accountant to do the budgets. Just remember, everyone has their own system for this, so no judging!

This budget is for a 30-minute TV game show with a total of 35 episodes. If this were a studio show, it would be broken down into:

Pattern Budget: What each episode costs
Amortization Budget: The startup of the show and the build, in which the sets are created
Wrap Budget: For the final week of the show
Dark Budget: Days when there is no shoot but the production staff and/or editing team is still working (let's say a show shoots four days a week and there's no filming on the fifth day – that's a dark day)
Hiatus Budget: For the time of the year when the show isn't in production, before filming picks up again for the following season – there's a skeleton crew during this period

You won't start using this, except for coding, until you're a production accountant. By then, you'll have taken all the classes you need and learned as much as you can (right?).

REGULAR IRS FRINGE RATES AND CORRESPONDING CEILINGS (to be set up in Movie Magic Budgeting)

media services
Feature / TV / New Media Payroll Rates 2020

HANDLING FEES	CA	NY
BTL Crew and Staff	1.25% of gross pay*	1.25% of gross pay*
Talent, Loanouts, other ATL	$14 flat per check	$14 flat per check

WORKERS' COMPENSATION		
Talent and Crew	4.03% on max $2,575/wk ATL	3.32% on max $5,725/wk
Editorial / Clerical	1.96%	2.06%
Overseas Production	7.72% on max $2,575/wk	7.72% on max $5,725/wk

FRINGES		
OASDI	6.2% on max $137,700/year	6.2% on max $137,700/year
Medicare	1.45%	1.45%
FUTA	0.6% on max $7,000/year	0.6% on max $7,000/year
SUTA	6.2% on max $7,000/year	7.9% on max $11,600/year
BTL Crew Total	19.73%	20.72%
ATL / Talent Total	18.48% + $14/check	19.47% + $14/check

INCLUDED AT NO ADDITIONAL COST	
• TiM Digital Onboarding	• MediaWeb Production Accounting System
• Showbiz Software products	• ACA tracking and Health Benefits Administration
• Mobile Timecards	• Incentives assistance

IMPORTANT NOTES

· San Francisco Expense Tax = 0.38%   · New York MTA Employer Tax = 0.34%

* Minimum fee per check is $5.00.

Please also note that all pay items (kit rentals, mileage, etc.) are subject to handling fees. Workers' Comp rate is applied to straight time rate of all hours worked – i.e., there is no premium on the Workers' Comp fee for Overtime incurred. SUTA and Workers' Comp subject to change per governmental and insurance carrier adjustments. **Note:** CA SUTA due on all CA residents.

mediaservices.com

Reprint courtesy of Media Services Payroll

BLANK NON-UNION EXTRA TALENT VOUCHER

NON UNION Extra Talent Voucher

DATE WORKED _____

PRODUCTION TITLE _____

EMPLOYEE: PLEASE *PRINT* NAME AND SIGN BELOW.
ALSO MAKE SURE ALL INFORMATION REQUIRED ON THE REVERSE SIDE IS COMPLETED.

NAME _____

S.S.# _____ PHONE # _____

E-MAIL ADDRESS _____

AFFORDABLE CARE ACT EMPLOYMENT BASIS *(MUST CHECK ONE)*:
☐ FULL TIME ☐ PART TIME ☐ VARIABLE HOUR ☐ SEASONAL

EMPLOYMENT ENDED ☐ NO ☐ YES DATE _____

SPECIAL UNPAID LEAVE: FROM: _____ TO _____

COMMENTS _____

SIGNATURE _____

CLIENT COPY

PLEASE ENTER TIMES BELOW: I HAVE WORKED ON THIS PICTURE BEFORE ☐

START TIME	MEAL PERIOD IN	MEAL PERIOD OUT	STOP TIME	HOURS WORKED
APPROVED FOR PAYMENT				

BASE RATE **TOTAL**

ACCT. #		hrs. @ S.T.	
		hrs. @ 1 1/2 x	
		hrs. @ 2 x	
MEAL PENALTY			

ADJUSTMENTS

STAND IN			
SMOKE			
PHOTO DOUBLE			
SILENT BIT			

ADJUSTMENTS

AUTO / MILEAGE REIMBURSEMENT			
WARDROBE REIMBURSEMENT			
MISC. REIMBURSEMENT			

GROSS AMOUNT

175

COMPLETED NON-UNION EXTRA TALENT VOUCHER

NON-UNION Extra Talent Voucher

DATE WORKED October 26, 2018

PRODUCTION TITLE Production Accounting: The Movie

EMPLOYEE: PLEASE PRINT NAME AND SIGN BELOW.
ALSO MAKE SURE ALL INFORMATION REQUIRED ON FORM W-4 BELOW IS COMPLETED.

NAME Thee X. Traguy   HIRE DATE 10/25

FITTING ☐   INTERVIEW ☐   MEALS B ☐ L ☐ D ☐

S.S.# 000-00-0000   PHONE # N/A - Uses carrier pidgeons

E-MAIL ADDRESS N/A - Uses carrier pidgeons   LOCATION ZIP CODE

AFFORDABLE CARE ACT EMPLOYMENT BASIS (MUST CHECK ONE):
☐ FULL TIME ☐ PART TIME ☐ VARIABLE HOUR ☐ SEASONAL

EMPLOYMENT ENDED ☐ NO ☐ YES DATE _____

SPECIAL UNPAID LEAVE: FROM _____ TO _____

COMMENTS

SIGNATURE _____ Imagine a really awesome signature

I HAVE WORKED ON THIS PICTURE BEFORE ☐

PLEASE ENTER TIMES BELOW:

START TIME	MEAL PERIOD IN	MEAL PERIOD OUT	HOURS WORKED	STOP TIME	TRAVEL TIME ARRIVE	TYPE OF CALL	TRAVEL TIME
10.0	14.0	14.8	7.2	18.0		N/A	N/A

APPROVED FOR PAYMENT N/A

BASE RATE

TYPE OF WORK	HOURS	RATE	ACCOUNT NUMBER	TOTAL
Background	7.2	$20/hour		$144.00
MILEAGE REIMBURSEMENT				
WARDROBE REIMBURSEMENT				
MISC. REIMBURSEMENT				
		GROSS AMOUNT		$144.00

TYPE OF WORK   D = DAY   N = NIGHT   W/S = WET/SMOKE   A = ADJUSTMENT

BLANK UNION EXTRA TALENT VOUCHER

Union Extra Talent Voucher ☐ I HAVE WORKED ON THIS PROJECT BEFORE

Work Location
City & Zip Code

DATE	PRODUCTION COMPANY AND TITLE		FULL SOCIAL SECURITY NUMBER (REQUIRED FOR PAYMENT)
LAST NAME	FIRST NAME	MIDDLE NAME/INITIAL	SAG-AFTRA ID#
ADDRESS			EMAIL ADDRESS
CITY	STATE/PROVINCE	ZIP CODE/POSTAL CODE	PHONE NUMBER

☐ FITTING ☐ INTERVIEW ☐ STAND-IN ☐ BACKGROUND ACTOR ☐ SPECIAL ABILITY ☐ PHOTO DOUBLE ☐ OTHER

TIME RECORD

REPORTING TIME	
SET DISMISSAL	
TOTAL HOURS	
FIRST MEAL OUT	
IN	
SECOND MEAL OUT	
IN	
TOTAL MEALS	
NET HOURS WORKED	

FOR ACCOUNTING/PRODUCTION USE ONLY

TYPE OF WORK

	WAGES					ALLOWANCES		
	PAY CODE	HOURS		RATE	AMOUNT		PAY CODE	AMOUNT
		WORK				Props		
Day						Auto		
1.5x						Mileage		
2x						Adjustment		
Wet/Smoke						Meal Penalty		
Hair/Makeup						Other		
Wardrobe								

TOTALS

BASIC RATE	
ADJUSTMENTS	
OVERTIME/MPV	
ALLOWANCES	
TOTAL GROSS	

AFFORDABLE CARE ACT EMPLOYMENT BASIS *(MUST CHECK ONE)*:
☐ FULL TIME ☐ PART TIME

EMPLOYMENT ENDED ☐ NO ☐ YES DATE _____

SPECIAL UNPAID LEAVE: FROM _____ TO _____

PLEASE READ THE FOLLOWING BEFORE SIGNING

By signing this voucher, I acknowledge and agree to the following:
(1) I agree to accept the sum properly computed based on the time and the basic wage rate shown as payment in full for all services heretofore rendered by me for said employer.
(2) I hereby give and grant to the company named, its successors, assignees, licensees or any other person or company who might gain title or rights to the Production, all rights of every kind and character whatsoever in and to all work heretofore done, and all poses, acts, plays by me for you and in to all of the results and proceeds of my services heretofore rendered for you, as well as in and to the right to use my name, likeness and photographs, either still or moving, for commercial and advertising purposes. I further give and grant to the said company the right to reproduce in any manner whatsoever, including by altering, clothing, editing and/or otherwise changing, any recordations hereto-

APPROVED FOR PAYMENT:

fore made by said company of my voice and all instrumental, musical, or other sound effects produced by me. I further agree that in the event of a retake of all or any of the scenes in which I participate, or if additional scenes are required (whether originally contemplated or not), I will return to work and render my services in such scenes at the same basic rate of compensation as that paid to me for the original taking. All such rights granted by me herein are to be worldwide and in perpetuity.

CA personnel: We have a Medical Provider Network (MPN) for all work-related injuries and/or illnesses. In the event of an injury, your care will be directed to a physician within the MPN. You may qualify to pre-designate a doctor. For more information, please contact us at 310.440.9675 or visit@mediaservices.com.

SIGNATURE: _____

COMPLETION OF FEDERAL & STATE FORMS REQUIRED

Reprint courtesy of Media Services Payroll

COMPLETED UNION EXTRA TALENT VOUCHER

Union Extra Talent Voucher

DATE	10/26
PRODUCTION COMPANY AND TITLE	Accounting Rocks, LLC.
Work Location City & Zip Code	Accountingland, 99955
I HAVE WORKED ON THIS PROJECT BEFORE	[ ]
FULL SOCIAL SECURITY NUMBER (REQUIRED FOR PAYMENT)	0 0 0 - 0 0 - 0 0 0 0
LAST NAME	Extra
FIRST NAME	Happ
MIDDLE NAME/INITIAL	E
(Title)	Production Accounting: The Movie
SAG-AFTRA ID#	some numbers between 0-9
ADDRESS	10001 Barren Cave St.
EMAIL ADDRESS	happ.e.extra@gmail.com
CITY	Desert Island
STATE/PROVINCE	CA
ZIP CODE/POSTAL CODE	00001
PHONE NUMBER	due to my religious beliefs, I don't believe in phones

[ ] FITTING [ ] INTERVIEW [ ] STAND-IN [X] BACKGROUND ACTOR [ ] SPECIAL ABILITY [ ] PHOTO DOUBLE [ ] OTHER

TIME RECORD

REPORTING TIME	8:00 AM
SET DISMISSAL	6:00 PM
TOTAL HOURS	10.0 hrs
FIRST MEAL OUT	1:00 PM
FIRST MEAL IN	1:30 PM
SECOND MEAL OUT	
SECOND MEAL IN	
TOTAL MEALS	30 min
NET HOURS WORKED	9.5 hrs

FOR ACCOUNTING/PRODUCTION USE ONLY

TYPE OF WORK	PAY CODE	WAGES WORK	RATE	AMOUNT
Day		8.0	$21.75	$174
1.5x		1.5	$32.625	$48.9475
2x				
Wet/Smoke				
Hair/Makeup				
Wardrobe				

ALLOWANCES	PAY CODE	AMOUNT
Props		
Auto		
Mileage		
Adjustment		
Meal Penalty		
Other		

TOTALS	
BASIC RATE	$174/8 hr
ADJUSTMENTS	
OVERTIME/MPV	$48.9475
ALLOWANCES	
TOTAL GROSS	$222.94

AFFORDABLE CARE ACT EMPLOYMENT BASIS (MUST CHECK ONE):
[X] FULL TIME [ ] PART TIME [ ] VARIABLE HOUR [ ] SEASONAL
EMPLOYMENT ENDED [ ] NO [ ] YES DATE _____
SPECIAL UNPAID LEAVE: FROM _____ TO _____

PLEASE READ THE FOLLOWING BEFORE SIGNING

By signing this voucher, I acknowledge and agree to the following:
(1) I agree to accept the sum properly computed based on the time and the basic wage rate shown as payment in full for all services heretofore rendered by me for said employer.
(2) I hereby give and grant to the company named, its successors, assignees, licensees or any other person or company who might gain title or rights to the Production all rights to the use of the results and proceeds of my services work heretofore done, and all poses, acts, plays by me for you and in all of the results and proceeds of my services heretofore rendered for you, as well as in and to the right to use my name, likeness and photographs, either still or moving for commercial and advertising purposes. I further give and grant to the said company the right to reproduce in any manner whatsoever including by altering, dubbing, editing and/or otherwise changing, any recordations hereto-fore made by said company of my voice and all instrumental, musical or other sound effects produced by me. I further agree that in the event of a retake of all or any of the scenes in which I participate, or if additional scenes are required (whether originally contemplated or not), I will return to work and render my services in such scenes at the same basic rate of compensation as that paid to me for the original taking. All such rights granted by me herein are to be worldwide and in perpetuity.

APPROVED FOR PAYMENT: _____ UPM/LINE PRODUCER'S SIGNATURE

SIGNATURE: _Happ E. Extra's Signature_

COMPLETION OF FEDERAL & STATE FORMS REQUIRED

Reprint courtesy of Media Services Payroll

Note, our extra has a rate of $174 per eight hours of work. Therefore, their time-and-a-half rate is calculated: ($174/8) x 1.5 = $32.625. This is a union extras voucher; the non-union voucher does not require a SAG-AFTRA ID.

BLANK CALIFORNIA LABOR CODE SECTION 2810.5 FORM

California Labor Code Section 2810.5   Rev. 07-27-2016
Written Notice and Acknowledgement of Pay Rate and Designated Payday
Effective January 1, 2012, the California Wage Theft Prevention Act of 2011, Labor Code section 2810.5(a) requires that ALL NON-EXEMPT employees be given written notice of their regular rate of pay, wage status and designated payday at time of hire. Any non-exempt employee working under a Collective Bargaining Agreement (CBA) does not need to be given a written notice if the CBA underscores terms for wages, hours of work and working conditions of the employee as well as provides premium wage rates of all OT hours worked and a regular rate of pay no less than 30% over the state minimum wage. For production employees, a written notice must be provided for each project on which the employee is hired.

Production Co./Employer _____ EIN (Optional) _____

Check all that apply: ☐ Sole Proprietor   ☐ Corporation   ☐ Limited Liability Company   ☐ General Partnership

Other name Employer is doing business as (if applicable): _____

Physical address _____ City _____ State ____ Zip _____ Phone (___) ___ - _____

Mailing address _____ City _____ State ____ Zip _____ Phone (___) ___ - _____

Payroll Company _____

Address _500 S. Sepulveda Blvd., 4th Floor_   City _Los Angeles_ State _CA_   Zip _90049_ Phone _(310)_ 440 - 9600

Workers' Compensation Insurance Carrier __Arch Insurance Company (administered by Broadspire)__

Address _P.O. Box 14352_   City _Lexington_   State _KY_ Zip _40512-4352_ Phone _(310)_ 440 - 9691

Employee Name _____ E-mail Address _____

Address _____ City _____ State _____ Zip_____

Your Job/Occupation Category is _____ Hire Date _____

Project Name (Job) / Number _____

Non-Exempt Employees: Regular rate(s) of pay $_____ per hour. Overtime rate(s): 1 ½ x per hour _____. 2 x per hour _____

Additional regular rate(s) of pay per hour or premium overtime rate(s) (provide specifics): _____

Employment agreement is: ☐ Oral ☐ Written

Allowances Taken: ☐ None ☐ Meals _____ per meal ☐ Lodging _____ ☐ Other _____

Designated Payday _____ ☐ Weekly ☐ Bi-Weekly ☐ Other _____ if more frequent.

Notice Given: ☐ At Hiring ☐ Before a change in pay rate(s), allowances claimed, or payday.

Employee Acknowledgement of Receipt:

Employee Signature _____ Date: _____

Production Co. Signature _____ Date: _____

Labor Code section 2810.5(b) requires that the employer notify you in writing of any changes to the information set forth in this notice within seven (7) calendar days after the time of the changes, unless one of the following applies: (a) All changes are reflected on a timely wage statement furnished in accordance with Labor Code section 226; (b) Notice of all changes is provided in another writing required by law within seven (7) days of the changes. The full text of Labor Code section 2810.5 may be found at www.leginfo.ca.gov/calaw.html. Check "Labor Code" and search for "2810.5" in quotes.

The employee's signature on this notice merely constitutes acknowledgement of receipt. In accordance with an employer's general recordkeeping requirements under the law, it is the employer's obligation to ensure that the employment and wage-related information provided on this notice is accurate and complete. Furthermore, the employee's signature acknowledging receipt of this notice does not constitute a voluntary written agreement as required under the law between the employer and employee in order to credit any meals or lodging against the minimum wage. Any such voluntary written agreement must be evidenced by a separate document.

This notice form is an adaptation of the template notice form issued by the CA DLSE on December 29, 2011 which may be found at www.dir.ca.gov/DLSE. This notice form is made available as an aid to be in compliance with the CA Labor Code section 2810.5(a). It is not intended as legal advice or as a substitute for review by legal counsel.

A signed copy to be provided to the employee and payroll company. Original should be retained by the production company/employer for at least 3 years.

Reprint courtesy of Media Services Payroll

COMPLETED CALIFORNIA LABOR CODE SECTION 2810.5 FORM

California Labor Code Section 2810.5   Rev. 07-27-2016
Written Notice and Acknowledgement of Pay Rate and Designated Payday

Effective January 1, 2012, the California Wage Theft Prevention Act of 2011, Labor Code section 2810.5(a) requires that ALL NON-EXEMPT employees be given written notice of their regular rate of pay, wage status and designated payday at time of hire. Any non-exempt employee working under a Collective Bargaining Agreement (CBA) does not need to be given a written notice if the CBA underscores terms for wages, hours of work and working conditions of the employee as well as provides premium wage rates of all OT hours worked and a regular rate of pay no less than 30% over the state minimum wage. For production employees, a written notice must be provided for each project on which the employee is hired.

Production Co./Employer Accounting Rocks, LLC   EIN (Optional) _____

Check all that apply: ☐ Sole Proprietor   ☐ Corporation   ☑ Limited Liability Company   ☐ General Partnership

Other name Employer is doing business as (if applicable): _____

Physical address 54321 Exciting Drive City Happyland State CA Zip 99992 Phone (555) 555 - 5552

Mailing address 98765 Thrilling Drive City Funkytown State CA Zip 99993 Phone (555) 555 - 5553

Payroll Company Awesome Payroll Company

Address 1225 Numbers Ln City Numbersland State CA Zip lots of 9s Phone carrier pigeons only

Workers' Compensation Insurance Carrier Great Workers' Insurance

Address some witty sounding address City clever city State CA Zip 041289 Phone smoke signals only

Employee Name Joe Schmoe E-mail Address joe.schmoe.999@gmail.com

Address 12345 Boring Lane City Chinatown State CA Zip 99955

Your Job/Occupation Category is Accounting Hire Date October 25, 2019

Project Name (Job) / Number Production Accounting:The Movie

Non-Exempt Employees: Regular rate(s) of pay $ 0714 per hour. Overtime rate(s): 1 ½ x per hour 1071 2 x per hour 1428

Additional regular rate(s) of pay per hour or premium overtime rate(s) (provide specifics): _____

Employment agreement is: ☐ Oral ☑ Written

Allowances Taken: ☑ None ☐ Meals _____ per meal ☐ Lodging _____ ☐ Other _____

Designated Payday End of the week ☑ Weekly ☐ Bi-Weekly ☐ Other _____ if more frequent.

Notice Given: ☑ At Hiring ☐ Before a change in pay rate(s), allowances claimed, or payday.

Employee Acknowledgement of Receipt:

Employee Signature Joe Schmoe's Signature Date: 10/25

Production Co. Signature Producer's Signature Date: 10/25

Labor Code section 2810.5(b) requires that the employer notify you in writing of any changes to the information set forth in this notice within seven (7) calendar days after the time of the changes, unless one of the following applies: (a) All changes are reflected on a timely wage statement furnished in accordance with Labor Code section 226; (b) Notice of all changes is provided in another writing required by law within seven (7) days of the changes. The full text of Labor Code section 2810.5 may be found at www.leginfo.ca.gov/calaw.html. Check "Labor Code" and search for "2810.5" in quotes.

The employee's signature on this notice merely constitutes acknowledgement of receipt. In accordance with an employer's general recordkeeping requirements under the law, it is the employer's obligation to ensure that the employment and wage-related information provided on this notice is accurate and complete. Furthermore, the employee's signature acknowledging receipt of this notice does not constitute a voluntary written agreement as required under the law between the employer and employee in order to credit any meals or lodging against the minimum wage. Any such voluntary written agreement must be evidenced by a separate document.

This notice form is an adaptation of the template notice form issued by the CA DLSE on December 29, 2011 which may be found at www.dir.ca.gov/DLSE. This notice form is made available as an aid to be in compliance with the CA Labor Code section 2810.5(a). It is not intended as legal advice or as a substitute for review by legal counsel.

A signed copy to be provided to the employee and payroll company. Original should be retained by the production company/employer for at least 3 years.

Reprint courtesy of Media Services Payroll

BLANK MILEAGE FORM

MILEAGE RECORD

NAME: _____

LAST 4 OF SSN: _____

JOB NAME/NUMBER _____

Date	Destination	Odometer Readings	Mileage

Total Miles = _____
X _____ cents per mile = _____

Total Amount _____

Reprint courtesy of Media Services Payroll

COMPLETED MILEAGE FORM

MILEAGE RECORD

NAME: Joe Schmoe

LAST 4 OF SSN: 6789

JOB NAME/NUMBER Assistant Accountant

Date	Destination	Odometer Readings	Mileage
10/25	Staples	100,000 start - 100,010 end	10
10/25	Filming Location	100,010 start - 100,050 end	40
10/25	Staples	100,050 start - 100,060 end	10
10/25	Bank	100,060 start - 100,075 end	15

Total Miles = 75

X 58 cents per mile = 43.50

Reprint courtesy of Media Services Payroll

Total Amount $43.50

If an employee doesn't complete this form, they will be taxed on their mileage reimbursements. The current mileage rate per the IRS is 58 cents a mile. Always double-check this (https://www.irs.gov/newsroom/irs-is-sues-standard-mileage-rates-for-2020), as it changes every couple of years.

BLANK PO (FRONT)

ACCOUNTING PRODUCTIONS
9800 Hollywood Way, #303
Los Angeles, CA 90254
P: (310) 222-7777

PO# 001000

DATE _____

SHOW NAME: _____

VENDOR:	_____	TAX ID # _____
ADDRESS:	_____	INCORPORATED: YES NO
ADDRESS:	_____	**W9 ON FILE?** YES NO
CONTACT:	_____	

REQUESTED BY:	DEPARTMENT
PURCHASE	TERMS:
RENTAL FROM: TO:	DAILY WEEKLY MONTHLY EXTENDED
DEPOSIT REQUIRED: AMOUNT _____	DATE RETURNED _____

** QUOTE OR INVOICE FROM VENDOR MUST BE ATTACHED**

CODE	DESCRIPTION	QUANTITY	PER UNIT	SUBTOTAL	TOTAL
Total					$

BUDGET NOTES:

APPROVAL

Executive in Charge of Production
Date:

APPROVAL:

DEPT HEAD
DATE: _____

LINE PRODUCER
DATE: _____

ACCOUNTANT
DATE: _____

By signing this purchase order I acknowledge that all related party transactions have been disclosed (if any) and were approved by the Executive in Charge of Production. If related parties exist, please disclose below.

_____

WHITE/ACCOUNTING   PINK/VENDOR   YELLOW/DEPARTMENT

W9 REQUIRED FOR PAYMENT

COMPLETED PO (FRONT)

ACCOUNTING PRODUCTIONS
9800 Hollywood Way, #303
Los Angeles, CA 90254
P: (310) 222-7777

PO# 001000
DATE 11/07/2019

SHOW NAME: Accounting rocks

VENDOR:	ABC COSTUMES RENTAL		TAX ID #	12-3456789	
ADDRESS:	11111 RIVERSIDE DR.		INCORPORATED:	YES	NO
ADDRESS:	N.HOLLYWOOD, CA 91504		W9 ON FILE?	YES	NO
CONTACT:					

REQUESTED BY:	Debbie	DEPARTMENT	Wardrobe

PURCHASE				TERMS:			
RENTAL	FROM: 10/2	TO: 10/21		DAILY	WEEKLY XXXX	MONTHLY	EXTENDED

DEPOSIT REQUIRED:			
AMOUNT	1,000.00	DATE RETURNED	10/22/2019

** QUOTE OR INVOICE FROM VENDOR MUST BE ATTACHED**

CODE	DESCRIPTION	QUANTITY	PER UNIT	SUBTOTAL	TOTAL
	Male western wear	4	allow	4000.00	4000.00
Total					$4,000.00

BUDGET NOTES:	Vendor requesting a 1,000.00 deposit

APPROVAL

Executive in Charge of Production
Date:

APPROVAL:

DEPT HEAD	LINE PRODUCER	ACCOUNTANT
DATE:	DATE:	DATE:

By signing this purchase order I acknowledge that all related party transactions have been disclosed (if any) and were approved by the Executive in Charge of Production. If related parties exist, please disclose below.

WHITE/ACCOUNTING   PINK/VENDOR   YELLOW/DEPARTMENT

W9 REQUIRED FOR PAYMENT

BLANK DRAW SHEET (BACK OF PO)

INVOICE WITH APPROVAL STAMP

DEBBIE NOLAN

1234 Alphabet Dr. Apt. ABC
Los Angeles, Ca 65478

TO: THE ACCOUNTANT

Invoice 0058

Date	To	Sent To
04/23/18		

Services

Hours	Description	Unit Price	Total
REIMB. OOOP	OFFICE DEPOT_OFF SUPPLIES	$	110.00
	EXCESS BAGGAGE FEE	$	200.00
	STAPLES_OFFICE SUPPLIES	$	128.33
		$	-
	SPLIT WITH XPS_CITW	$	-
		$	-
		$	-
		$	-
USD		$	-
		$	-
		$	-
	TOTAL	$	438.33

Thank you for your business!

APPROVAL STAMP	
PO #	4568
CODING	3615
(OV)/UNDER C	
LP APPVL	
ACCT. APPVL	PTB
AMT LEFT ON PO	NO PO

THE CLERK

BLANK W-9

| Form **W-9**
(Rev. October 2018)
Department of the Treasury
Internal Revenue Service | **Request for Taxpayer
Identification Number and Certification**

▶ Go to *www.irs.gov/FormW9* for instructions and the latest information. | **Give Form to the
requester. Do not
send to the IRS.** |

1 Name (as shown on your income tax return). Name is required on this line; do not leave this line blank.

2 Business name/disregarded entity name, if different from above

3 Check appropriate box for federal tax classification of the person whose name is entered on line 1. Check only **one** of the following seven boxes.

☐ Individual/sole proprietor or single-member LLC ☐ C Corporation ☐ S Corporation ☐ Partnership ☐ Trust/estate

☐ Limited liability company. Enter the tax classification (C=C corporation, S=S corporation, P=Partnership) ▶ _____

Note: Check the appropriate box in the line above for the tax classification of the single-member owner. Do not check LLC if the LLC is classified as a single-member LLC that is disregarded from the owner unless the owner of the LLC is another LLC that is **not** disregarded from the owner for U.S. federal tax purposes. Otherwise, a single-member LLC that is disregarded from the owner should check the appropriate box for the tax classification of its owner.

☐ Other (see instructions) ▶

4 Exemptions (codes apply only to certain entities, not individuals; see instructions on page 3):

Exempt payee code (if any) _____

Exemption from FATCA reporting code (if any) _____

(Applies to accounts maintained outside the U.S.)

5 Address (number, street, and apt. or suite no.) See instructions.

Requester's name and address (optional)

6 City, state, and ZIP code

7 List account number(s) here (optional)

Part I Taxpayer Identification Number (TIN)

Enter your TIN in the appropriate box. The TIN provided must match the name given on line 1 to avoid backup withholding. For individuals, this is generally your social security number (SSN). However, for a resident alien, sole proprietor, or disregarded entity, see the instructions for Part I, later. For other entities, it is your employer identification number (EIN). If you do not have a number, see *How to get a TIN*, later.

Social security number

Note: If the account is in more than one name, see the instructions for line 1. Also see *What Name and Number To Give the Requester* for guidelines on whose number to enter.

or

Employer identification number

Part II Certification

Under penalties of perjury, I certify that:

1. The number shown on this form is my correct taxpayer identification number (or I am waiting for a number to be issued to me); and
2. I am not subject to backup withholding because: (a) I am exempt from backup withholding, or (b) I have not been notified by the Internal Revenue Service (IRS) that I am subject to backup withholding as a result of a failure to report all interest or dividends, or (c) the IRS has notified me that I am no longer subject to backup withholding; and
3. I am a U.S. citizen or other U.S. person (defined below); and
4. The FATCA code(s) entered on this form (if any) indicating that I am exempt from FATCA reporting is correct.

Certification instructions. You must cross out item 2 above if you have been notified by the IRS that you are currently subject to backup withholding because you have failed to report all interest and dividends on your tax return. For real estate transactions, item 2 does not apply. For mortgage interest paid, acquisition or abandonment of secured property, cancellation of debt, contributions to an individual retirement arrangement (IRA), and generally, payments other than interest and dividends, you are not required to sign the certification, but you must provide your correct TIN. See the instructions for Part II, later.

Sign Here | Signature of U.S. person ▶ | Date ▶

General Instructions

Section references are to the Internal Revenue Code unless otherwise noted.

Future developments. For the latest information about developments related to Form W-9 and its instructions, such as legislation enacted after they were published, go to *www.irs.gov/FormW9*.

Purpose of Form

An individual or entity (Form W-9 requester) who is required to file an information return with the IRS must obtain your correct taxpayer identification number (TIN) which may be your social security number (SSN), individual taxpayer identification number (ITIN), adoption taxpayer identification number (ATIN), or employer identification number (EIN), to report on an information return the amount paid to you, or other amount reportable on an information return. Examples of information returns include, but are not limited to, the following.

• Form 1099-INT (interest earned or paid)

• Form 1099-DIV (dividends, including those from stocks or mutual funds)

• Form 1099-MISC (various types of income, prizes, awards, or gross proceeds)

• Form 1099-B (stock or mutual fund sales and certain other transactions by brokers)

• Form 1099-S (proceeds from real estate transactions)

• Form 1099-K (merchant card and third party network transactions)

• Form 1098 (home mortgage interest), 1098-E (student loan interest), 1098-T (tuition)

• Form 1099-C (canceled debt)

• Form 1099-A (acquisition or abandonment of secured property)

Use Form W-9 only if you are a U.S. person (including a resident alien), to provide your correct TIN.

If you do not return Form W-9 to the requester with a TIN, you might be subject to backup withholding. See What is backup withholding, later.

Cat. No. 10231X   Form **W-9** (Rev. 10-2018)

COMPLETED W-9

Form **W-9** (Rev. November 2017) Department of the Treasury Internal Revenue Service	**Request for Taxpayer Identification Number and Certification** ► Go to *www.irs.gov/FormW9* for instructions and the latest information.	Give Form to the requester. Do not send to the IRS.

1 Name (as shown on your income tax return). Name is required on this line; do not leave this line blank.
CHARLIE DRIVEMAN

2 Business name/disregarded entity name, if different from above
N/A

3 Check appropriate box for federal tax classification of the person whose name is entered on line 1. Check only **one** of the following seven boxes.

[✓] Individual/sole proprietor or single-member LLC [ ] C Corporation [ ] S Corporation [ ] Partnership [ ] Trust/estate

[ ] Limited liability company. Enter the tax classification (C=C corporation, S=S corporation, P=Partnership) ► _____

Note: Check the appropriate box in the line above for the tax classification of the single-member owner. Do not check LLC if the LLC is classified as a single-member LLC that is disregarded from the owner unless the owner of the LLC is another LLC that is **not** disregarded from the owner for U.S. federal tax purposes. Otherwise, a single-member LLC that is disregarded from the owner should check the appropriate box for the tax classification of its owner.

[ ] Other (see instructions) ►

4 Exemptions (codes apply only to certain entities, not individuals; see instructions on page 3):

Exempt payee code (if any) _____

Exemption from FATCA reporting code (if any) _____

(Applies to accounts maintained outside the U.S.)

5 Address (number, street, and apt. or suite no.) See instructions.
12345 MAIN ST.

6 City, state, and ZIP code
CHARLIELAND, CA, 98393

Requester's name and address (optional)

7 List account number(s) here (optional)

Print or type.
See Specific Instructions on page 3.

Part I Taxpayer Identification Number (TIN)

Enter your TIN in the appropriate box. The TIN provided must match the name given on line 1 to avoid backup withholding. For individuals, this is generally your social security number (SSN). However, for a resident alien, sole proprietor, or disregarded entity, see the instructions for Part I, later. For other entities, it is your employer identification number (EIN). If you do not have a number, see *How to get a TIN*, later.

Note: If the account is in more than one name, see the instructions for line 1. Also see *What Name and Number To Give the Requester* for guidelines on whose number to enter.

Social security number

| 1 | 2 | 3 | – | 4 | 5 | – | 6 | 7 | 8 | 9 |

or

Employer identification number

| | | – | | | | | |

Part II Certification

Under penalties of perjury, I certify that:

1. The number shown on this form is my correct taxpayer identification number (or I am waiting for a number to be issued to me); and
2. I am not subject to backup withholding because: (a) I am exempt from backup withholding, or (b) I have not been notified by the Internal Revenue Service (IRS) that I am subject to backup withholding as a result of a failure to report all interest or dividends, or (c) the IRS has notified me that I am no longer subject to backup withholding; and
3. I am a U.S. citizen or other U.S. person (defined below); and
4. The FATCA code(s) entered on this form (if any) indicating that I am exempt from FATCA reporting is correct.

Certification instructions. You must cross out item 2 above if you have been notified by the IRS that you are currently subject to backup withholding because you have failed to report all interest and dividends on your tax return. For real estate transactions, item 2 does not apply. For mortgage interest paid, acquisition or abandonment of secured property, cancellation of debt, contributions to an individual retirement arrangement (IRA), and generally, payments other than interest and dividends, you are not required to sign the certification, but you must provide your correct TIN. See the instructions for Part II, later.

Sign Here	Signature of U.S. person ►	CHARLIE DRIVEMAN	Date ►	FEBRUARY 32, 2019

General Instructions

Section references are to the Internal Revenue Code unless otherwise noted.

Future developments. For the latest information about developments related to Form W-9 and its instructions, such as legislation enacted after they were published, go to *www.irs.gov/FormW9*.

Purpose of Form

An individual or entity (Form W-9 requester) who is required to file an information return with the IRS must obtain your correct taxpayer identification number (TIN) which may be your social security number (SSN), individual taxpayer identification number (ITIN), adoption taxpayer identification number (ATIN), or employer identification number (EIN), to report on an information return the amount paid to you, or other amount reportable on an information return. Examples of information returns include, but are not limited to, the following.

• Form 1099-INT (interest earned or paid)

• Form 1099-DIV (dividends, including those from stocks or mutual funds)

• Form 1099-MISC (various types of income, prizes, awards, or gross proceeds)

• Form 1099-B (stock or mutual fund sales and certain other transactions by brokers)

• Form 1099-S (proceeds from real estate transactions)

• Form 1099-K (merchant card and third party network transactions)

• Form 1098 (home mortgage interest), 1098-E (student loan interest), 1098-T (tuition)

• Form 1099-C (canceled debt)

• Form 1099-A (acquisition or abandonment of secured property)

Use Form W-9 only if you are a U.S. person (including a resident alien), to provide your correct TIN.

If you do not return Form W-9 to the requester with a TIN, you might be subject to backup withholding. See What is backup withholding, later.

Cat. No. 10231X   Form **W-9** (Rev. 11-2017)

BLANK PETTY CASH COVER

ACCOUNTING ROCKS
THE 123 OF NUMBERS
PC COVER

ENVELOPE # _____

EMPLOYEE: _____ PROJECT: _____ THE 123 OF NUMBERS

ADDRESS: ON FILE _____ DATE SUBMITTED: _____

LOCATION _____ DATE RECONCILED: _____

DATES: _____ TO: _____ APPROVED BY: _____

DATE	#	PAYEE	DESCRIPTION	ASSET	CODING	AMOUNT
	1					
	2					
	3					
	4					
	5					
	6					
	7					
	8					
	9					
	10					
	11					
	12					
	13					
	14					
	15					
	16					
	17					
	18					
	19					
	20					
	21					
	22					
	23					
	24					
	25					
	26					
	27					
	28					
	29					
	30					
	31					
	32					
	33					
	34					
	35					
	36					
	37					
	38					
	39					
	40					
	41					
	42					
					GRAND TOTAL:	0.00

ACCOUNT NAME	ACCT #	AMOUNT	ACCOUNT NAME	ACCT #	AMOUNT
SCRIPT COPIES	1185				
CASTING EXPENSES	1415				
CRAFT SERVICE SUPPLIES	2515				
LUNCH	3620				
FUEL	3544				
PARKING &NMETERS	3632		**PROJECT NAME**	**CODE**	**AMOUNT**
			THE 123 OF NUMBERS		0.00
			ACCTG ROCKS		0.00

COMPLETED PETTY CASH COVER

ACCOUNTING ROCKS
THE 123 OF NUMBERS
PC COVER

ENVELOPE # _____ PB0001 _____

EMPLOYEE: PENELOPE B	PROJECT: THE 123 OF NUMBERS
ADDRESS: ON FILE	DATE SUBMITTED: 1/1/2020
LOCATION LOS ANGELES	DATE RECONCILED:
DATES: 12/15/2020 TO: 12/30/2019	APPROVED BY:

DATE	#	PAYEE	DESCRIPTION	ASSET	CODING	AMOUNT
12/15/19	1	OLIVE GARDEN	CREW LUNCH		3620	125.00
12/18/19	2	CHEVRON	FUEL		3544	45.80
12/21/19	3	KINKOS	COPIES		1185	55.00
12/26/19	4	RALPHS	ICE CREAM		2515	40.25

GRAND TOTAL: 266.05

ACCOUNT NAME	ACCT #	AMOUNT	ACCOUNT NAME	ACCT #	AMOUNT
SCRIPT COPIES	1185	55.00			
CASTING EXPENSES	1415				
CRAFT SERVICE SUPPLIES	2515	40.25			
LUNCH	3620	125.00			
FUEL	3544	45.80			
PARKING &NMETERS	3632		PROJECT NAME	CODE	AMOUNT
			THE 123 OF NUMBERS		266.05
			ACCTG ROCKS		0.00

PAYROLL CHEAT SHEET (CREATED IN EXCEL)

Production Accounting: The Movie

Start Date	Position	Last	First	SS	Code	Loan Out	Guarantee	Salary	Hourly	1.5	2	40 hrs	Per Diem	Box	Start	State
	DIRECTOR/PRODUCERS															
	Director/Writer															
	Line Producer															
	Co-Producer															
	Co-Producer															
	Co-Producer															
	ACCOUNTING															
	Production Accountant															
	Assistant Accountant	Schmoe	Joe	6789	1205	N/A	12	$1.00	0.0714	0.1071	0.1429	2.86	Yes			
	PRODUCTION STAFF															
	UPM															
	POC															
	APOC															
	1st AD															
	2nd AD															
	2nd 2nd AD															

EXTRAS SKIN

EXTRAS SKINS

Date:			Friday				
#	Name	Phone Number	Email	Role		Rate	CALL
01	Dan "The" Man	888-888-8888	xtras@gmail.com	Cook		$174/8	12:00PM
02	Mabido Soises	888-888-8888	xtras@gmail.com	Dishwasher		$174/8	12:00PM
03	Jomez Goyana	888-888-8888	xtras@gmail.com	Hostess		$174/8	12:00PM
04	Allen Kemist	888-888-8888	xtras@gmail.com	Smelter		$174/8	12:00PM
05	Tim Timmerson	888-888-8888	xtras@gmail.com	Pedestrian		$174/8	9:15AM
06	Pete Peterson	888-888-8888	xtras@gmail.com	Pedestrian		$174/8	9:15AM
07	Walt Walterson	888-888-8888	xtras@gmail.com	Pedestrian		$174/8	9:15AM
08	NO MORE NAMES	888-888-8888	xtras@gmail.com	Man dressed as Penguin		$174/8	2:00PM

The End

You've done it. You've read the book. You've mastered the jargon. You weren't scared off by the paperwork – in fact, you kinda liked looking at all those forms. You've decided you were right... you *do* want to become a production accountant. Hurray!

Now, it's time to call all the different payroll companies. Talk to the marketing departments and the tech departments to schedule your first online classes for the different software and introduce yourself as a clerk.

Once you've done that, add that knowledge to your resume.

THEN SELL YOURSELF!

YOU CAN DO IT.

A final note: You won't get everything right on your first job. Mistakes are going to happen. Crew members are going to be paid late, checks are going to be cancelled and reissued, files are going to be lost. It is inevitable.

You should be commended for purchasing and reading a book on production accounting. It proves you are driven and motivated to either enter the world of production accounting or fine-tune your accounting skills. If you only take away one thing from this book, remember that if you're a hard worker, you're organized, you pay attention to detail, you recognize that things are not always going to go as planned, and you don't talk back and think you know more than the other people in the office do, you will be fine. I guarantee it.

Best of luck and thanks for reading. I really hope my book has helped you.

See you out there!

Glossary

1099
Forms a vendor receives at the end of the year if they are being paid as an individual and no taxes are being taken out.

Accounts Payable (A/P)
Money owed by a business to its suppliers, shown as a liability on a company's balance sheet.

Accounts Receivable (A/R)
The balance of money due to the production for services delivered or used but not yet paid for by studio or employee, including bill backs. It varies from show to show, and not every studio will allow it. Example: Let's say Ford wants us to shoot an opening spot for 15 seconds. We then create an A/R account and all the cost for the spot will be coded to that account, and then we send an invoice out to Ford for them to pay the bill.

Asset
Property owned by a person or company, regarded as having value. Ask your studio finance person what the minimum dollar amount is for an item to be tracked as an asset.

Background Artist

A performer in a film or television show who appears in a non-speaking or non-singing role in the background (for example, in an audience or a busy street scene). In production accounting paperwork, these performers are referred to as extras.

Bank Reconcile

The process of matching the production's accounts with the production's bank statements. Like balancing a checkbook. This is done monthly.

Bible

A detailed report by accounting of what has been spent.

Bill Backs

Costs that the studio or production company covers before the show as an entity is set up, which then have to be reimbursed by the show. These costs could be for writers, studio overhead, or other labor.

Box Rental Form

A form listing the items an employee or contractor is renting to the show. These can be things like cell phones, laptops, printers, and so on, and a box rental must always be approved by production. Submitted weekly.

Call Sheet

Created by the assistant director, this is a daily schedule based on the director's shot list. It is issued to the cast and crew of a film production to inform them of where and when they should report for a particular day of filming, what the director intends to shoot that day, when lunch is, and so forth.

Cash Flow

A report that gives the weekly breakdown of what the production needs to spend for the run of the show. The accountant makes a detailed cash flow report and then a weekly summary cover to attach to the forms given to production for the week. Tweak as you go.

Check Register
This is a list of all checks written to date, generated by the accounting software.

Cost Report
A report that tells the studio or production company how much the production has spent to date. These are due every week while shooting, and the accountant turns in a final one when the production wraps. In post-production, cost reports are delivered either every two weeks or monthly, depending on whether or not the show is on track financially.

Credit One-Sheet
A one-sheet with all of the production company's information to help open accounts. See sample in Chapter 13.

Daily Production Report (DPR)
The form filled out each day of production on a movie or television show to summarize what occurred that day.

Day Out of Days (DOOD)
A chart used by productions to let everyone know what days the items or actors will be working; see the example on page 151. The chart must be prepared after the shooting schedule is drafted. Once it has been completed, work can begin on creating a budget.

Deal Memo
A contract between a crew member and the production company that lays out the crew member's rate for salary. This can be a weekly or hourly salary, and it may include a stipulated sixth-day rate, the number of hours the person is guaranteed for the day, and any rentals the person is being paid for.

Estimate to Complete
The column on the cost report that details how much money remains in the budget for each code.

Exempt
An employee who is compensated at a fixed rate rather than by the hour, usually someone high on the food chain. They are "exempt" from hourly rates and pay hour calculations. It isn't necessary to break time cards for exempt employees.

Exhibit G
A time report — simply a daily record of each performer's time on set. It's a pretty straightforward form used to fill out the actor's time card.

Extra
Technically, a performer in a commercial who appears in the same capacity as a background actor in a TV show or film — but in production accounting, we use this term for all shows, not just commercials.

Hot Cost
A daily report created by the production accountant to let the producers know the overages or underages of the previous day's work.

Integration Costs
Costs when a show is sponsored by a product. For example, Nissan gives the show $125,000 to be featured in a particular segment. The accountant or first will allocate a code for the show to use for anything that pertains to that segment's costs. Your show has an opening red-carpet sequence with a Nissan in the background? Any cost pertaining to that is coded separately.

Journals
These are usually kept for funding or coding corrections. A journal entry top sheet should be attached to each journal you create and enter.

Loan-Out
Someone working for the production not as a sole contractor but as an owner/employee of a legal business entity established for the purpose of providing that contractor's personal services to third parties.

MICR
Acronym that stands for Magnetic Ink Character Recognition and refers to the special numbers at the bottom of checks that include the account number, bank routing number, check number, etc. Both MICR ink and MICR toner are used to print these numbers on checks.

Mileage Form
A form where an employee logs the miles for each journey they make for the production.

Non-Affiliate
A contract specifically for production accountants and assistant accountants hired out of New York or California and working for one of the five major studios, in which they can get most union benefits without belonging to the accountants' union (IATSE). Not all union perks are paid, but the most important ones are, like insurance and 401(k).

Non-Deductible Break
When a crew member, cast member, or extra is given a walking meal in between lunch and dinner but the time is not deducted from their hours worked. It's to avoid meal penalties, which incur if lunch doesn't begin within six hours of the call time or there are more than six hours between the end of lunch and wrap.

Non-Exempt
An employee who is compensated by the hour, usually below-the-line crew and staff members. They are not "exempt" from pay hour calculations or labor laws, and you will be breaking their time cards for payroll.

Pay Hours

See page 56 for a detailed explanation.

Petty Cash (PC)

A cash float issued to employees at the start of the show so they can buy what they need to make the show happen — wardrobe, props, craft service, etc. They turn in a PC envelope every week so the PC they have spent can be replaced and they can have the same amount available for production needs the following week.

P-Cards

A form of company charge card that allows the holder to procure goods and services without using a traditional purchasing process.

PC Envelope

A cover sheet with all of the holder's petty cash receipts documented on it and totaled. See page 13.

Per Diem

A daily cash allowance established by the production company to cover meals while on location. Meals provided as part of a food allowance are counted separately from per diem.

Production Manager (PM)

Organizes the business, finance, and employment issues on all productions. The PM is in charge of how the production budget is spent and making sure that everything runs smoothly during filming.

Purchase Order (PO)

This needs to be filled out by department heads and turned in when they make purchases or rentals or have a Loss and Damage item. These help to track costs. POs are very important because you'll use them to determine whether there is enough in the relevant account to cover an invoice.

Skin Sheet
A top sheet for the daily stack of extras vouchers, detailing the extras' names, rates of pay, and whether they were general background or in specialized roles, such as stand-ins, photo doubles, or performers with special skills.

Trial Balance
A report that lets you and the studio know who has PC, P-cards, deposits, and A/R.

W-9
Used in the United States income tax system by a third party who must file an information return with the IRS. It requests the name, address, and taxpayer identification information of a taxpayer (in the form of a Social Security number or employer identification number). W-9s are never sent to the IRS, but are maintained by the production, which files the information return for verification purposes.

Workers' Compensation (WC)
A form of insurance providing wage replacement and medical benefits to employees injured in the course of employment.

Resources

Here is a list of resources to help you along. Many of these apply specifically to productions based in California, so if you're based elsewhere, you may need to do a little more digging on your own — but sources are out there for you, I promise!

You can also contact the film offices local to you to get an idea of what's available in your city and state.

Payroll Companies
These companies all offer training on their software.

ENTERTAINMENT PARTNERS
Ep.com

CAST AND CREW
Castandcrew.com

GREENSLATE
gslate.com

ABS PAYROLL
Abspayroll.com

MEDIA SERVICES
www.mediaservices.com

ENTERTAINMENT MEDIA SERVICES
www.emspayroll.com

Entertainment Classes

UCLA
Extension classes, perfect for the part-time student in you
https://www.uclaextension.edu/entertainment

AMERICAN FILM INSTITUTE
https://www.afi.com

TALK FILM
Starts with a workshop, then moves into online study
http://www.talkfilm.biz/index.html

Payroll Classes

SMART ACCOUNTING SOLUTIONS
http://www.smartaccountingsolutions.com

ENTERTAINMENT PARTNERS
Enrichment classes
https://www.ep.com/courses

Books
Another great resource

The Complete Film Production Handbook, by Eve Light Honthaner
https://www.walmart.com/ip/The-Complete-Film-Production-Handbook

A to Z Guide to Film Terms, by Tim Moshansky
https://www.amazon.com/Z-Guide-Film-Terms-ebook/dp/B005I6V8DO/ref=dp_kinw_strp_I

Networking
Facebook pages for production accounting

https://www.facebook.com/groups/1420680558252725

https://www.facebook.com/groups/143961440154

https://www.facebook.com/groups/1462849103971567

https://www.facebook.com/groups/263105437134632

About Penelope Bunsen

Learn the secrets to a successful career in production accounting. Set yourself apart from other candidates by having first-hand knowledge from reading *Intro to Production Accounting: The Clerk* by Penelope Bunsen, an established accountant for over 20 years.

Andrea Simon
Executive in Charge of Production – Yellow Pad Productions

Having worked with Penelope over several years on various types of projects, I can say with confidence that she is very passionate about her work. Penelope adapts quickly to new personalities and takes everything in stride. I found Penelope always a step ahead and prepared to problem solve at a moment's notice. Production moves quickly, which can be a challenge for even the most seasoned professional. The attention to detail that I have found in Penelope's work is one of the many reasons I would welcome her on any project I may have.

Monica Stock
Senior Vice President of Production – Talpa

Penelope Bunsen is a perfectionist when it comes to television show accounting. She has created her own techniques over the years which have proven to account, track, and forecast show budgets. Regardless of the size of the budget, her proven approach of controlling and communicating costs expenditures has enabled producers like myself to put more money on screen. With tightening budgets and more pressure than ever to deliver an extremely high-quality product, knowing where you stand financially every step of the way during the production and post-production process is essential, and Penelope has proven that show after show.

Tony Yates
Executive Producer of *The Challenger* – GateKeeper Productions, Inc.

Printed in Great Britain
by Amazon

14655451R00119